Triple Value

With the sustainability emergency, businesses can no longer give priority to commercial interests (and financial gains) and close their eyes to societal and environmental interests. We need a new, higher perspective to close the gap. We need to formulate a new business logic and a sustainable value creation method for sustainable business, for their customers and society – that is, all business stakeholders, as well as the planet. This book will do just that.

This book presents the insights gained from action research with leading companies across the world to discover a comprehensive method that works: a practical framework for CEO and business leaders who want to lead their organization along the sustainability transition. Building on the latest insights from science, summarized as the systems view of life, the book identifies six principles that provide a new leadership lens on how to understand the changes taking place in business and create sustainable value from a systems perspective. Based on these insights, the book offers the Triple Value mindset model, consisting of six distinct leadership qualities, to enable business leaders to scale their intended impact from the organization to all stakeholders in the value chain, thus transcending the conflict between business and society.

Not only that, the book will also offer you a leadership journey – an adventure that will transform the way to think, feel and execute the new perspective in your company, while perfecting your leadership potential and inspiring the people you work with. On the journey you will be supported by models, tools and best practices, which will help you to reimagine your business strategy and your role as leader in driving sustainable transformation and success.

Sander Tideman is a specialist in leadership development and organizational transformation, motivated by building the capacity to address the unprecedented social and ecological challenges of this age. Tideman is founder of Triple Value Leadership, and associated to the Garrison Institute, Mobius Executive Leadership and Rotterdam School of Management, Erasmus University.

Triple Value Leadership

Creating Sustainable Value for Your
Business, Your Customers and Society

Sander Tideman

Routledge
Taylor & Francis Group

LONDON AND NEW YORK

Cover image: flashgun / Getty Images

First published 2022
by Routledge
4 Park Square, Milton Park, Abingdon, Oxon OX14 4RN

and by Routledge
605 Third Avenue, New York, NY 10158

Routledge is an imprint of the Taylor & Francis Group, an informa business

British Library Cataloguing-in-Publication Data
A catalogue record for this book is available from the British Library

Library of Congress Cataloging-in-Publication Data
Names: Tideman, Sander, author.
Title: Triple value leadership : creating sustainable value for your business, your customers and society / Sander Tideman.
Description: 1 Edition. | New York, NY : Routledge, 2022. |
Includes bibliographical references and index. |
Identifiers: LCCN 2021053403 (print) | LCCN 2021053404 (ebook) |
ISBN 9780367634469 (hardback) | ISBN 9780367634780 (paperback) |
ISBN 9781003119302 (ebook)
Subjects: LCSH: Leadership. | Organizational change.
Classification: LCC HD57.7 .T5223 2022 (print) |
LCC HD57.7 (ebook) | DDC 658.4/092–dc23/eng/20211123
LC record available at https://lccn.loc.gov/2021053403
LC ebook record available at https://lccn.loc.gov/2021053404

ISBN: 978-0-367-63446-9 (hbk)
ISBN: 978-0-367-63478-0 (pbk)
ISBN: 978-1-003-11930-2 (ebk)

DOI: 10.4324/9781003119302

Typeset in Adobe Garamond
by Newgen Publishing UK

Contents

Figures

Acknowledgments

There are a great number of people who I want to thank.

First and foremost, my research partner Muriel Arts for co-initiating and coleading the research project over the last decade. Her optimistic outlook and visionary drive encouraged me greatly. I am grateful to Prof. Dr. Rob van Tulder and his colleagues of Rotterdam School of Management, Erasmus University, who supported this project wholeheartedly, thanks to a grant from the Netherlands Science Research Council. I am also indebted to Dan Nixon and Maarten Wubben for providing valuable editorial comments to earlier versions of the manuscript. I thank my agent Pim van Tol, as well as Rebecca Marsh and Chrissy Mandizha of Taylor & Francis for making this publication possible.

There are a number of scholars and teachers who I met personally and who provided invaluable insights that have shaped this book: the Dalai Lama, Chogyam Trungpa, Hazel Henderson, Fritjof Capra, Alan Wallace, Joe Loizzo, Michael Porter, David Cooperrider, Daniel Siegel, Miki Walleczek, Daniel Goleman, Annie McKee, Erica Fox, Richard Barrett, Peter Senge, Herman Wijffels and Otto Scharmer.

I am also indebted to my colleagues Amy and Erica Fox (Mobius Executive Leadership), Diana and Jonathan Rose (Garrison Institute), Amy Cohen-Varela (Mind & Life Europe), Piero Overmars, Danielle Zandee, Jaap van Muyen and the late Paul de Blot (Nyenrode Business University), as well as all my other friends who supported and encouraged me: Anders Ferguson, Marcello Palazzi, Reinout van Lennep, John van Giels, Chamutal Eitam Afek, Henk Schulte Nordholt, Volkert Engelsman, Peter Blom, Wieke Janssen, Jeroen Smit, Jeroen Drontmann, Barend van Dam, Florens van Canstein, Reinier Tilanus, Titus Bekkering, Chiel van Kollenburg, Tanno Bregonje, Linda van Aken, Sue Cheshire, Chris Tamdjidi, Ricardo Sunderland, Pepijn van der Meulen, Hans Vriens and Hans Reus.

Last but not least, I am grateful to the many business leaders who have been subject of our research and shared valuable insights from their business practice – most are mentioned in the book.

Through Triple Value Foundation we are continuing our research. We welcome you to join us in sharing your stories and experiences, so as to create a community of practice of leaders who generate Triple Value. Together we can help transform capitalism toward a system of value creation that serves life on this planet. You can contact us at www.triplevalueleadership.com.

I would like to close with a quote of biologist Francisco Varela, "This world is our dance together – not my projection, not yours. It's something we do together, and what we do changes what the world is like".

Introduction

In the last few years, we have seen a tipping point in the role of business in society: with the growing planetary crisis, attacks on democracy and the ongoing health challenge, business can no longer give priority to commercial interest and financial gains at the expense of societal and environmental interests. Leaders in business and society will now need to develop a new and higher perspective to align the needs of society and the environment with the commercial interests of business. Business will not flourish unless people and the planet are flourishing.

The quest for such higher perspective has motivated me throughout my career. I started my work with degrees in international economic law and Asian affairs with an interest in the emerging markets of Asia. I was fascinated by how countries such as Japan, South Korea and Taiwan, who were considered part of the "third world", suddenly leaped from the third to the first world in a matter of years, becoming known as the so-called Asian tigers. After training at the law firm Baker & McKenzie in Taiwan, I worked for ABN AMRO Bank as chief representative for China, with postings in Hong Kong, Beijing and Shanghai.

This unique experience in Asia, which spanned the entire 1990s, gave me insight into the mechanics of booming globalization, but I also witnessed its shadow. When countries open up to global capitalism, their ecosystems tend to disintegrate and social inequality flares up – inevitable by-effects of economic growth. I also experienced firsthand the destabilizing effects of the Asian financial crisis of 1998 and the Internet bubble crash some years later, foreshadowing the global financial meltdown a decade later. While I had seen the benefits of globalization and the liberalization of markets, the unchecked and speculative force of capital that followed disturbed me deeply. How could business bring sustainable benefit to these countries, if the system supporting business was unsustainable by nature?

This question got more persistent year-by-year. With the world facing growing societal and ecological challenges from climate change, resource depletion, pandemics, mass immigration and disruptive technology, many business leaders whom I met did not know how to respond to these challenges. I felt that too many leaders were hooked onto "business as usual", which did not make sense in a world that was rapidly moving into the unusual. How can leaders in business think that

DOI: 10.4324/9781003119302-1

they can be successful when the societies and ecosystems that they depend on are on the verge of collapse?

I decided not to despair and look for solutions. While no doubt business is part of the problem, I did not want to see it *merely* this way. Rather, I wanted to know how business could become part of the solution. So I shifted my career to the field of sustainable finance and investment, while pursuing a parallel career in research and teaching.

This shift coincided with the rise of Corporate Social Responsibility (CSR) initiatives in business. Many CSR efforts were placed at the margin of the core business, leading to the publication of nicely looking social reports and business philanthropy, but little was done to integrate sustainability into the core strategy of business. In fact, I believed that the way CSR was framed was setting business up for failure: if companies would accept that there was something like "socially responsible" business aside from their normal business, they logically also needed to accept that their normal business was "socially *irresponsible*" business.

Indeed, I saw many businesses continue with negatively impacting our natural and social environment by causing pollution, depleting vital resources and promoting unhealthy lifestyles – in spite of paying lip service to CSR. The CSR movement brought a multitude of exotic terms into the board room – Environmental Social Governance, Ecological Footprint, Triple Bottom Line, Cradle-to-Cradle, Circular Economy, Impact Entrepreneurship, Stakeholder Capitalism and many others – but how do all these concepts hang together? Which of them are mission critical?

What's worse, some companies started to use these terms in their business communication to pretend that all was well, or to find clever ways of luring customers, which is known as *green washing*. Likewise, business leaders started to speak about *purpose* to indicate that they are serving a higher goal than just making money. However, when their actions do not match their words, these statements amount to *purpose washing*.

The "how" of sustainable business transformation

My journey across the sustainability world convinced me that something more fundamental was needed. If CSR is not the answer, then what is it? Something that would appeal to business logic, that would indicate that sustainability is not a cost issue per se, but an inevitable investment into a change process that would bring multiple long-term benefits, including financial ones.

If real change was to be achieved, sustainability should be at the heart of business logic. The main thing missing, in my opinion, is the understanding of *how* companies can step up to this challenge and move in the right direction. How can the supertanker of business transform itself, so that companies no longer merely *extract* value, but start to *create* value for the needs of society and the planet? How can companies become net benefactors to society and the environment, while still also benefiting themselves? How can we transform capitalism from "within"?

In the role of consultant for organizations such as the World Bank, International Finance Corporation (IFC) and Triodos Bank, I traveled the world in search of companies that were leading in sustainability fields such as renewable energy, organic food and microfinance. I discovered that authentic sustainable companies are led by leaders with distinct qualities: they are committed to a vision for a sustainable world, while having the ability to build a successful and profitable organization.

These could be for-profit companies with a social purpose or not-for-profit organizations with a business orientation. What they had in common was a model of value creation for more stakeholders than the owners alone – in fact, they were creating "shared value" for themselves and society. In these companies, there was no apparent conflict between the needs of core business and the needs of society.

Their leaders had transcended the common dilemma of social benefit versus profits, expressing this in (somewhat awkward) terms such as "social enterprise" or "purpose-based business".

On a global level, I sensed that if we want to create a sustainable economic system, we need to radically reorient our leadership from merely creating profits to creating value for society. If we want to divert the machine of global capitalism from its self-destructive course, we will need courageous leaders who are equipped to change direction. This became the heart of my quest: to create this type of new leadership – sustainable leadership.

I specialized my research and work in leadership development, studied with leading scientists of the mind, delved deeply in contemplative practice and co-created a global leadership network. I worked with senior business leaders and their teams on finding purpose and sustainable high performance. Gradually, a vision emerged of what sustainable leadership entails and how it could be practiced.

Triple Value research project

Nyenrode Business University in the Netherlands offered me a platform to explore and test my emerging ideas. When I met Muriel Arts, a fellow researcher in sustainability with an extensive track record in international business and brand strategy, innovation and marketing, we decided to join up and establish the Triple Value Foundation as a vehicle to engage in action research with companies and their leaders.

Later, thanks to Professor Rob van Tulder of the Rotterdam School of Management, Erasmus University, we received a grant for our research from the Netherlands Science Research Council.

Over a period of several years, we studied and worked with many different companies and interviewed hundreds of executives. We also conducted an extensive review of literature in the fields of sustainability, strategy, leadership and organizational transformation and performance, as well as the more fundamental sciences of behavioral economics, biology, sociology and psychology. Our end goal was to develop a comprehensive method for business leadership that works, spanning the dimensions of leadership, strategy and performance management.

We concentrated our research on firms that are considered leading companies in sustainability. Some are listed on the Dow Jones Sustainability Index and are earmarked by sustainability monitors and investors, but we also looked at smaller sustainability pioneers. Most of these firms are considered leading among their peers. Subsequently, we validated the methodology that we developed by working with a number of these companies.

We set out to discover *how* companies could embrace the challenge and opportunity that sustainability represents – and start solving the bigger societal problems that we face. It became the most ambitious but also the most rewarding project that we ever undertook. We were fortunate to work with truly remarkable leaders around the world. In the process, we became witness to a revolution-like change sweeping the business world, a major transition from CSR to entirely new value creation models.

Key insights that inspired us:

- Leading companies are transforming themselves toward sustainability. The *UN Sustainable Development Goals* have been embraced as a guiding framework by hundreds of companies, which together can shift global supply chains. Sustainability is a $12 Trillion a Year Market by 2030, while the cost of not acting on sustainability will cost us many times more.[1] Changing consumer demands, the rise of shareholder activism and a sea change in the sustainability regulatory landscape indicate that a tipping point has arrived – sustainability has become mainstream.

- Neuroscience, psychology, behavioral economics and branches of social science are developing new knowledge, indicating the prosocial nature of human beings, which uproot long-held assumptions behind economics, leadership and human potential. These insights discredit the material/mechanical view of economies and companies in favor of the *living systems view*, leading to a more holistic, generative and compassionate outlook on how we can create value for business and society.

- *Interconnectedness and interdependence* is not just a cool idea, but one of the underpinnings of successful global companies. They employ value-chain approaches, connecting all stakeholders in the value creation process, with an integrated performance model. This is giving rise to the concept of a "value network" or "value system".

- It is possible and necessary to redefine sustainability as a *"need" of markets, society and ecosystems*, and redefine business as agents to serve those needs. Only by serving real and tangible needs can "value" be created. This goes back to the basic principles of entrepreneurship and performance. More than 80% of Environmental, Social and Governance (ESG) funds (invested on sustainability principles) outperformed their benchmark.[2]

- Many leaders are waking up. Many of them are searching for a *deeper and shared purpose* to have an impact on the world. They are engaged in transformative practices, such as mindfulness, emotional intelligence and compassion, which help them to navigate complexity, behave differently and take more responsibility. Clear and balanced minds make better decisions and stay around longer.

• Sustainability is the next level in *leadership development*. Global executive recruiters will be screening the next CEO on their capacity to lead their companies into instruments for societal change. Sustainability, ethics, staff well-being and high performance are becoming connected in leading companies.

Taken together, these key insights provide the elements of a *new paradigm* that allow business leaders to positively contribute to society by recognizing that business is *a part of* society and not *apart from* society. This recognition profoundly alters the way business positions itself vis-à-vis society and will flip the business model from value extraction into joint value creation and reimaging business success. Rather than creating value primarily for the shareholders and senior managers, business can now learn to create value for their organizations, their customers *and* society at the same time – this is what we call *Triple Value*.

Many entrepreneurs start with good intentions – very few of them *would not want* to create value for all their stakeholders. At the same time, living up and keeping such intention turns out to be difficult and rare. Why is this so? Why are so many companies locked in a strategy of trade-offs, between profits and principle, often caught in a race to serve the bottom line – while the ecological bottom is rapidly approaching as well?

The answer is painfully simple: we use *outdated ways of thinking*: we hold on beliefs, leadership styles, strategies, vested interests and performance models that may have worked in the past, but are no longer fit for purpose. The world has changed, and the purpose of business now needs to change as well.

The promise of this book

The research project generated a wealth of information, providing exciting answers to the "how" question of sustainable business transformation. These answers allowed us to formulate a new theory on value creation – Triple Value creation (TVC). The new TVC theory has ramifications on business strategy, leadership, innovation, marketing and performance management.

This book will focus on the big picture of Triple Value, while making it relevant for *business leadership*. It will show you how to *think differently* in order to create a truly sustainable business. This is not merely theoretical: we will provide you with case studies and practical tools along the way.

This book has three parts. The first part (*Why*) will start with a historical overview to show the current business paradigm is under siege. The many sustainability efforts taking place in business cannot stand up against a system that runs on principles of the industrial machine model: maximizing material growth, supply and demand, and efficiency of invested capital. We will call this the *Growth Triangle*.

The problem is that the underlying assumptions of the Growth Triangle cannot comply with the sustainability demands of today. Likewise, we can no longer assume that free markets will regulate themselves and naturally evolve to a healthy equilibrium, as the classical economic dogma led us to believe.

We are facing a systems shift: the current economic model is moving to a model that serves the needs of all stakeholders and respects the boundaries of the planet. The new model goes under different names: stakeholder capitalism, circular economy, green growth or regenerative economics – to name but a few. In terms of metaphors, we see the Triangle of Growth transforming into the *Circle of Sustainability*.

The Circle of Sustainability can be understood at three interrelated levels: the larger economic system, business organizations and the beliefs we hold about ourselves – in short: *System, Organization, Self* (SOS), an acronym that helps us to remind the urgency of this work.

Part 1 will conclude with the review of the related shift in science, which indicates that we are moving away from a purely material/mechanical worldview to an alternative yet more accurate and life-affirming worldview that can be called the *systems view of life*. From this review, I will identify the *six principles* that define and sustain life, whether it is an organism, a company or an ecosystem. In this book, I will apply these six principles of life onto the three levels of SOS. This will provide the structure for the narrative of the book.

In Part 2 (*What*), I will apply these principles to the way we should manage economic system and companies – which are (contrary to earlier assumptions) subject to how living systems operate. This new view provides an empowering perspective on shifting business toward genuine sustainability. Indeed, we conclude that this corresponds to what leading companies are actually doing, which represents an entirely new stage in business sustainability – *the stage of TVC.*

Beyond changes at the system and business level, the underlying beliefs and mindsets of people will have to change as well. Most of us have been conditioned for decades to believe that economies are designed for economic growth and that the prime purpose of business is to make money. This is no longer accurate and – worse – it is misleading and dangerous in times of accelerating environmental destruction and social inequality.

If we don't change the mindsets of people, we will continue to be confused about the role of companies and economics. Business leaders will pay lip service to sustainability, but inwardly still feel tied to the credo of the limited growth model. They will fall prey to pleasing outside stakeholders with wrong intentions. As a result, we will see a pandemic of inauthentic greenwashing.

Thus, Part 3 of the book (*How*) is dedicated to how leaders can make this change. It will offer the reader a new leadership lens on how to create sustainable value, transcending the conflict between business and society. It includes a *TVC leadership mindset model* representing the "systems mindset" needed for the systems' crisis that we are facing. The model consists of six succinct leadership qualities, which leaders will need to cultivate in order to address the complex challenges of today – at SOS levels.

Not only that: this book will also offer you a journey – an adventure that will transform the way to think, feel and act the new perspective in your organization. Essentially, I hope this book will inspire you to *reimagine* your leadership success. You don't have to feel powerless in the face of an increasingly uncertain and complex world and settle for unsatisfactory trade-offs between the needs of your company and those of society and the planet.

The Triple Value perspective will help you to see that societal challenges are not to be feared; they can be your future growth markets where you can achieve sustainable impact. They can also help you to transform your company into a purpose-driven organization that attracts the right people, clients and resources. By actually serving the growing needs of the planet and society, you can become a *brand of choice* for consumers, *the preferred employer* for future talent and be on the *top of the list* of the growing community of impact investors.

Most importantly, this presents an opportunity for you to become the courageous leader who actually makes a difference in these unprecedented times – not only winning with your business but also winning with society and the planet.

I hope that this book will help to change the way we perceive ourselves and the world. This change presents a new paradigm of leadership in business and society: *Triple Value Leadership*.

Notes

1 Elkington, J. European Business Review, October 20, 2017 Issue.
2 Polman, P., & Winston, A. (2021). The Net Positive Manifesto, Harvard Business Review.

Part 1

Why?

Why do we need a new approach to value creation?

Chapter 1

The challenges facing the business world

This chapter will explain how drastic changes in the environmental and societal context of business are posing a fundamental challenge to the sustainability of the current economic model. This current model is no longer equipped to deal with the unprecedented changes we are witnessing today, which is fueling a growing disconnect between business and society. We will look at the impact of the challenges, before recognizing that there are at the same time enormous opportunities for (sustainable) value creation as well.

We will see that the international response to this challenge – expressed in the Sustainable Development Goals – can only be successful if business becomes a proactive partner in the realization of these goals.

Unprecedented changes in the context of business

After the Second World War, society and business entered into a new "social contract": business was given a free reign in reconstructing the post-War world.[1] With the rapid globalization of the economy and technical and social innovation, business fully seized this opportunity by contributing to tremendous positive developments across the world. In all countries where business was given the purpose to create economic growth, we have witnessed substantial improvements in health and wealth, access to education and higher life expectancy – a big boost to the standard of living of humanity.

But the economic growth came at a price. Globalization ran parallel to the rise of the consumer culture, as mass consumerism became the main driver of growth,

DOI: 10.4324/9781003119302-3

which fueled an insatiable demand for more and more production, as well as run-away amounts of waste. Within the same period of time, more than half of the planet's ecosystems that support human well-being have been degraded and are used unsustainably.[2] This is compounded by the rise of a nationalist and popu-list politics that challenge the very system that has created so much improvement to our standard of living. People are not only polarized largely due to rising social inequality but also burnt out from a mental health epidemic like never before: it is estimated that 792 million people live with mental health disorder, mostly anxiety and depression. This is more than one in ten people globally.[3]

Given these fundamental challenges, the post-war social contract between business and society needs to be revised.[4] The economic growth paradigm *isn't working* well any more, and business will need to find a new purpose in its role in society.

Inequality threatens social cohesion and trust

In the West, even before the outbreak of the COVID-19 pandemic, stagnant incomes among a large part of the population caused people to be angry at elites. Large group of people feel victims of globalization; they see others get rich, not themselves. How much inequality is there really?

Since 1980, it is reported that the top 1% captured twice as much global income growth as the bottom 50%.[5] In 2018 the poorest half of the world became 11% poorer, while the wealth of billionaires rose 12% ($900 billion), which is $2.5 billion every day.[6] In comparison, almost half of the world population has to live on less than US$ 5.50 per day. The American economist Joseph Stiglitz stated, "40 per-cent of the world's wealth is controlled by 1 percent of the people".[7]

The story is a bit more complicated, as there is a difference between perceived and actual inequality, where perceived inequality is a more fundamental threat to political stability.[8] In any event, the International Monetary Fund (IMF) warned that inequality within nations has risen so sharply that it threatens to undermine economic growth and may well result in further political polarization.[9] Too many are left behind in a globalized world.

The ongoing technological innovations, the so-called fourth industrial revo-lution, may have created an amazingly connected world, with more than 50% of the world population having access to the Internet, yet it leaves many people also concerned about the future of work.[10] Elsewhere, too, people are losing out: either environmentally, such as the citizens of polluted cities, or socially, through the breakdown of traditional and rural communities.[11]

There are growing groups of citizens organized through social media that are very cynical about the current role of political and business elites across the entire polit-ical spectrum. They simply don't trust the current system anymore, as they witness a growing sense of inequality and unfairness in the system.

The Edelman Trust Barometer 2020 shows that a majority of people do not believe they will be better off in five years' time: "56% of respondents globally believe that capitalism in its current form is doing more harm than good in the world, while 66% don't believe that our current leaders will be able to successfully address our countries' challenges".[12]

Environmental degradation and climate change

Everywhere we can observe that economic development goes hand in hand with stark environmental degradation and climate change. On land, in the seas, in the sky, the devastating impact of human economic activity is laid bare. Scientific evidence also suggests that the apparition of new pathogens such as COVID-19 is linked with the continuing destruction of our biosphere,[13] the thin sphere around the planet, which provides all we need to for our life on earth.

The pandemic shows that this destruction of our biosphere is not merely damage to the environment: it is a direct attack on humanity as well. Planetary health and human health are interrelated. As the corona crisis has demonstrated, it has literally made the world sick. Separating the current global health and social crisis from the larger climate crisis would not make sense.

We slowly but surely destroy our natural habitats through deforestation, illegal wildlife trade, intensive agriculture and livestock production and global warming.[14]

And we can't deny that we have something to do with it. We hear much about climate change and extinction, but how bad is this really? Well, cutting-edge research has tried to summarize these threats in a "planetary boundary framework". It tracks where we are exceeding our limits. For example, one million animal and plant species are now close to extinction.[15] In 2050, our oceans will contain more plastic than fish. Some 30% of all food is wasted, while of all packaging, 91% becomes waste. Only 9% is used. Whether it is deforestation, air and water pollution, pandemics, global warming, plastic soup, chemicals in our food – they come as inevitable by-effects of globalized markets driven by our economic demands for ever more food, clothes and energy.[16]

Moreover, our planet simply has insufficient resources for unlimited financial and economic growth. Since our current economic indicators ignore the societal and ecological context in which businesses have to operate, we have reached a point that *the cost of not acting* for a sustainable world – containing food security, climate adaptation and mitigation, gender equality or epidemic prevention, to name a few basic human and planetary needs – becoming higher *than the cost of acting*. For example, the cost of conflict prevention and wars is estimated at 12% of global gross domestic product (GDP), whereas implementing the Sustainable Development Goals, the world's sustainable development agenda, only costs 3%–4% of GDP per year.[17]

"We are clearly the last generation that can change the course of climate change, but we are also the first generation with its consequences", says Kristalina Georgieva, Chairman of the IMF.

The invisible hand of the market – can we still trust it?

The model that has brought us here – known as "free-market capitalism" – has been the dominant organizing principle for economies for the last century. The system was based on a number of simple beliefs. Society can place its trust in the "invisible hand" of the market to deliver increased collective welfare. Companies were structured on the metaphor of a machine, with the CEO as chief engineer, managers as efficient soldiers, in pursuit of profit for shareholders. This mechanistic logic led to the idea to structure organizations centrally and hierarchically, with its typical control-oriented bureaucracy.

The invention of capital, the virtual form of money that can be endlessly leveraged, enabled shareholders to make "return on capital" the ultimate goal of the economic system.[18] Even though we may not learn this at school in exactly these terms, the machine metaphor operating in free self-regulating markets permeates much of our conventional thinking in business, economics, finance and even in politics, education and health care.

But now people ask: where is the invisible hand leading us? The logic dictates that nations should be generating GDP, just as the purpose of companies is to create shareholder value. However, by now we know that, after a certain threshold, there is no direct correlation between increasing GDP and well-being of citizens.[19] Money only helps with basic material needs, but beyond that does not create happiness. Moreover, our citizens are motivated by more than commercial value or money: we need belonging in family and community, healthy food, clean water, meaning, self-development and care, equality and trust in our social interactions – which are needs that the current shareholder value-based model doesn't recognize or steer upon.[20]

By relying blindly on the invisible hand of the market, we have failed to account for many of its *visible* side effects. What worked in the past does not work any longer.

As Marc Benioff, chairman and co-CEO of Salesforce, wrote in the New York Times: "Capitalism has been good to me. Yet, as a capitalist, I believe it's time to say out loud what we all know to be true: capitalism, as we know it, is dead".[21]

It is time to remove our blindfold. The economist Joseph Stieglitz noted: "There is nothing that guides our economic behavior except our own intentions and actions".[22]

Defining sustainable development

Now let's look at what can be changed. Many of the external sustainability threats are not new. In 1972, the Club of Rome generated headlines with its groundbreaking report "The Limits to Growth", which sold 30 million copies, making it the best-selling environmental book in history.[23] The 1973 oil crisis heightened public concern about the problem of resource depletion, but it was only in 1987 that a United Nations (UN) report captured this threat and defined its response in the term "sustainable development", which paved the way for coordinated action by the international community.[24] In 2000, the UN proclaimed the Millennium Development Goals (MDG's), which were eight international development goals to be reached in 2015. This was mainly led by multilateral government interventions, with the help of civil society, activists and NGOs, but critical stakeholders such as business were missing in action.

This omission was corrected when in 2015 the UN formulated the *17 Sustainable Development Goals (SDGs)*, or Global Goals, which were accepted by all member states in 2015, after an extensive consultative process, including all relevant stakeholders.[25] The idea behind the SDGs is that achieving them would result in a world that is fully sustainable, socially fair, environmentally secure, economically prosperous, inclusive and more predictable. This was historic; it was the first time in human history that the international community united as one front to formulate such a comprehensive, inclusive and far-sighted vision.

The main reason why the SDGs represent such a comprehensive view, and the most important difference between the MDGs and the SDGs, is that the latter have been made with and fully endorsed by global business. In fact, it was the first time that such a high-level political agenda was formulated with the active involvement of business leadership. To illustrate this, the SDGs incorporate the ten principles of the UN Global Compact, a guide to sustainable business behavior, to which over 9,000 companies around the world had already signed up.[26]

System: planetary boundaries

Tipping points are one of the scariest pieces of the emerging climate crisis. There are thresholds in our climate system that we must not cross. If we do, natural feedback loops could accelerate beyond our control and we'd end up with runaway warming and annihilated ecosystems. These are long-term, basically irreversible changes that would mean unimaginable amounts of devastation, suffering, and death for people and all life on earth.

The concept of planetary boundaries was proposed in 2009 by a group of 28 internationally renowned scientists led by Johan Rockström, director of the Stockholm Resilience Centre. They defined science-based planetary boundaries (such as climate change, biodiversity, wetlands, ocean acidification) that earmark a safe operating space that will allow humanity to continue to develop and thrive for generations to come.[27] These boundaries have been incorporated into the SDGs.

The importance of the concept of planetary boundaries comes to life when we link it to the SDG framework. The SDGs 6, 13, 14 and 15, ensuring a healthy biosphere, match the nine boundaries.

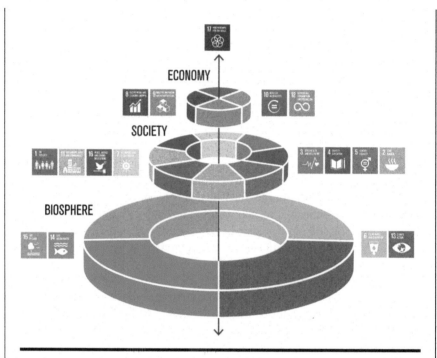

Figure 1.1 Planetary boundaries

The above model shows that these four SDGs constitute the safe planetary operating space of humanity to create a sustainable society and economy.[28] In other words, only when we achieve SDGs 6, 13, 14 and 15 do we stand a chance to obtain the other SDGs as well. It shows that these environmental SDGs are in a sense fundamental: a healthy biosphere is a precondition for a healthy society and economy.

The important role of business in sustainable development

The role of business in the context of the SDGs is more than endorsing it. The SDGs are built on the premise that business will be a key partner in the realization of the SDGs. According to the Business and Sustainable Development Commission (BSDC), set up for this purpose of engaging business around the goals, achieving the SDGs opens up US$12 trillion of market opportunities in mainly four economic systems.[29] These are food and agriculture, cities, energy and materials, and health and well-being. For example, we will need to decarbonize the other 70% of the world economy – steel, cement, transportation, fertilizer production and much more.

All this represents around 60% of the real economy, which is *an innovation effort on a scale the world has never seen before.* To capture these opportunities in full, the BSDC states that "businesses need to pursue social and environmental sustainability as avidly as they pursue market share and shareholder value".

These are crucial statements, which we will take forward in this book. In essence, if we want business to live up to the promise of the SDGs, the business will have to take an honest look at what it is doing to cause the problem and what it can do the solve it. Business can no longer leave the large sustainability challenges up to the governments or civil society to solve.

Factors impacting business growth

In fact, business has no choice but to take part, as many changes at the *macro level* translate directly into negative effects on the *micro level* of business. These effects are not "optional" as they cause a direct and immediate burden on business, affecting the profit and loss statement and balance sheet. They uproot business models *from within*, both at the production and demand side, enhancing the risk profile for investors and shareholders. A report by Accenture confirmed this trend: more and more business leaders and investors start to see that the sustainability agenda shapes the context within which business has to operate and many CEOs call for more action on corporate sustainability.[30]

In short, the stakeholders of the current value creation model need to brace themselves for impact. We will just mention the obvious and immediate challenges that they are facing.

Government regulations

At the moment, the economic system doesn't price in the real cost of pollution, such as using fossil fuels. Most users don't pay anything for the harm done to the environment by pollution from the fuel in their car or the coal or gas at home. This will change. Having committed to the SDGs and the Paris Climate Agreement, many nations are translating these commitments into hard laws, as well as new Environmental, Social and Governance (ESG) risk and return frameworks for monitoring investments. Specifically, companies can expect higher taxation on CO_2 emissions, use of water, chemicals and the disposal of waste. This will translate into price signals that will encourage the private sector to create green products.

In 2021, a series of events indicate that this is fast becoming the "new normal" for business, as our global interconnectedness becomes more and more manifest. On April 21, 2021, the European Commission adopted a proposal for a Corporate Sustainability Reporting Directive (CSRD) that radically improves the existing reporting requirements of the European Union's (EU) Non-Financial Reporting Directive. This ambitious package of measures will no doubt wake up the CFOs of business organizations to act on sustainability as well. The CSRD covers all relevant ESG elements and aims to increase investments in truly sustainable activities across the EU. This is also applicable to non-EU firms operating in Europe.[31]

In May 2021 a Dutch court ruled that Royal Dutch Shell must reduce net emissions by 45% by 2030, while Exxon Mobile Exxon shareholders turned on the board and elected directors demanding climate action. Chevron investors voted 61% in favor of a proposal to force the group to cut emissions. As Mark van Baal, founder of Follow This, who submitted this proposal, said, "Institutional investors understand that no investment is safe in a global economy ravaged by devastating climate change".[32] All this coming shortly after an International Energy Agency report saying investors should stop funding new oil, gas and coal projects if the world is to achieve net-zero emissions by 2050.

Consumers' preferences

Consumers are becoming more mindful in what they buy and consume, as evidenced by the rise of veganism and healthy food – a trend intensified as a result of the COVID-19 pandemic.[33] This ranges from health-conscious people to those concerned with animal welfare and land use negatively affected by industrial meat production, being conscious of air miles associated with imported food – for example, eating seasonal (local) fruit and veg, rather than imported blueberries from the other side of the world.

Issues such as equal pay, responsible production, local sourcing, responsible farming practices and child labor are moving to the forefront of the consumers' mind when making purchase choices. In an increasingly open and digitalized world, business must keep up with growing demands for ethical behavior and transparent reporting on issues such as employee rights, greenhouse gas emissions and the recycling of plastic.

Organization: Burger King

In October 2019, Burger King announced they would remove the plastic toys with children meals, after a campaign from two sisters aged 7 and 9, who were concerned about the ocean. Weeks earlier, the two sisters, Caitlin and Ella McEwan, started an online petition that got 510,000 signatures. They write online:

> We like to go to eat at Burger King and McDonald's, but children only play with the plastic toys they give us for a few minutes before they get thrown away and harm animals and pollute the sea. We want anything they give to us to be sustainable so we can protect the planet for us and for future generations.[34]

Burger King stated this will save 320 tonnes of plastic a year as a result of this campaign.

This example shows that ethical consumers, who can exercise their power not only through the products they buy but also through social media, will hold companies accountable.

Localization of supply chains

The COVID-19 crisis has placed a dent in global supply chains. A survey by the Institute for Supply Chain Management reported that a staggering 97% of organizations have been impacted by the COVID crisis.[35] The current model, with a focus on centralization, inventory reduction, cost saving and "just-in-time" delivery, has enabled us to build highly efficient yet also highly fragile global supply chains. Because of the focus on efficiency and centralization, they lack buffer capacity and resilience to absorb a supply chain disruption such as a pandemic. The efficiency-model leaves our supply chains painfully unprepared for disruptions on international trade. Moreover, supply chains are often long and convoluted, allowing social and environmental debacles such as slavery and ecocide to remain obscured, setting the stage for major reputational risks.[36]

Human resources

Business should be concerned about the shortage of human resources. Largely because of demographics and changing work–life needs, the lack of skilled talent will impact business performance in the years to come. The developed markets will be the hardest hit.[37] And what's more, this talent pool isn't very much motivated by mere financial incentives anymore. Research by LinkedIn indicates that a stunning 64.7% of top talent wants to work for companies with a purpose, taking care of the environment and the communities that they impact.[38] This is echoed in a survey by Deloitte, in which millennial workers were asked what the primary purpose of businesses should be – 63% more of them said "improving society" than "generating profit".[39]

Mark Carney, former Governor of the Bank of England, wrote: "Companies that don't adapt, including companies in the financial system, will go bankrupt, without question. But also there will be great fortunes made along this path aligned with what society wants".[40]

Disconnect between business and society

What this review shows is that the predominant belief that the Growth Triangle equals progress for all is misleading in significant ways: it has caused a growing disconnect between business and society. Business has outsourced the responsibility for society and nature to the public domain. In many places business has

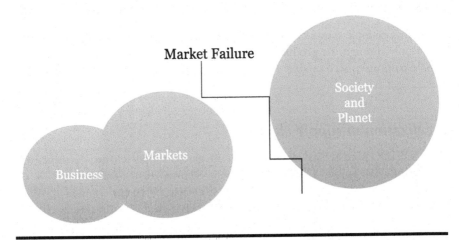

Figure 1.2 Disconnect between business/society and planet

become a powerful yet insular force, mainly extracting value from its context, gradually worsening the unsustainable situation that we find ourselves in. What is the purpose of business? Evidently, the traditional social contract has changed.[41]

The growing dichotomy between business and society is not just a problem for society: the social license of business is called into question. It is obvious that business, designed as the main mechanism to create value, should do much better than this. The growing disconnect between business and society does not only pose a challenge to public leadership but also to business leadership as well. The 2019 Edelman Trust Barometer says: "76 percent of people agree that CEO's should take the lead rather than waiting for governments to impose it – an 11 point increase from the 2018 Edelman study".[42]

Business needs to respond to the challenges in society and the environment in a different way than it has done in the last few decades – the "golden age" of free market globalization. Business needs to take ownership of what classical economists would call a *market failure*. Exhausting critical nature resources, disrupting ecosystem services and overloading the biosphere with climate change are by-effects of business activity and thus indicate a failure of the market to correct itself.

The view of separation between business, markets and society has become outdated and obsolete. Business should be seen as co-responsible for maintaining societal and environmental health and curtailing challenges such as runaway climate change, inequality, obesity, poverty, fresh water scarcity, to name a few. Obviously, this goes beyond just preventing market failures, and it is also about proactively instigating reform and transforming business practices and principles.

In short, if we want to heal the disconnect, we will need to see a fundamental transformation of *the dominant value creation paradigm of business*. This is what we will discuss in the following chapters.

Notes

1 Cragg, W. (2000). Human rights and business ethics: Fashioning a new social contract. In *Business Challenging Business Ethics: New Instruments for Coping with Diversity in International Business* (pp. 205–214). Springer, Dordrecht. Available online via: http://citeseerx.ist.psu.edu/viewdoc/download?doi=10.1.1.194.5854&rep=rep1&type=pdf.

2 UN Report by IPBES (Intergovernmental Science-Policy Platform on Biodiversity and Ecosystem Services, retrieved from www.un.org/sustainabledevelopment/blog/2019/05/nature-decline-unprecedented-report/.

3 Global Burden of Disease (2019) Institute for Health Metrics and Evaluation. Retrieved from: https://ourworldindata.org/mental-health [Online Resource].

4 Cragg, W. (2000). Human rights and business ethics: Fashioning a new social contract. In *Business Challenging Business Ethics: New Instruments for Coping with Diversity in International Business* (pp. 205–214). Springer, Dordrecht. Available online via: http://citeseerx.ist.psu.edu/viewdoc/download?doi=10.1.1.194.5854&rep=rep1&type=pdf.

5 World Inequality Lab, December 14, 2017 https://wir2018.wid.world/files/download/wir-presentation.pdf.

6 Oxfam Novib 2019 www.oxfam.org/en/research/extreme-carbon-inequality.

7 *New York Times*, February 17, 2019.

8 Hauser, O. P., & Norton, M. I. (2017). (Mis) perceptions of inequality. *Current Opinion in Psychology, 18*, 21–25.

9 Dunsmuir, L. (October 11, 2017). *IMF calls for fiscal policies that tackle rising inequality.* Reuters News.

10 AlphaBeta analysis for the Business and Sustainable Development Commission. Based on data from: Institute for Economics and Peace, 2015. *Global Peace Index 2015.* Available at: http://economicsandpeace. org/wp-content/uploads/2015/06/Global-Peace-Index-Report-2015_0.pdf.

11 Food and Agriculture Organization of the United Nations (FAO), 2015. *The impact of disasters on agriculture and food security.* Rome. Available at: www.fao.org/3/a-i5128e.pdf.

12 Edelman Trust Barometer 2020, January 19, 2020.

13 Christine, K. J., Peta, L. H., Pranav, S. P., Julie, R., Tierra, S. E., Cristin C. W. Y., & Megan M. D. *Global shifts in mammalian population trends reveal key predictors of virus spillover risk.* Proceedings of the Royal Society. Published: April 8, 2020. https://doi.org/10.1098/rspb.2019.2736.

14 www-bloomberg-com.cdn.ampproject.org/c/s/www.bloomberg.com/amp/news/articles/2020-04-08/want-to-stop-the-next-pandemic-start-protecting-wildlife-habitats.

15 UN Report (2019) Intergovernmental Science-Policy Platform on Biodiversity and Ecosystem Services (IPBES).

16 UN Report (2019) Intergovernmental Science-Policy Platform on Biodiversity and Ecosystem Services (IPBES).

17 Business and Sustainable Development Commission's analysis in their report "Better Business, Better World".

18 While money refers to cash items, capital is a bookkeeping term on the company's balance sheet. You can have capital without cash, as long as you have more creditors (loans) than debtors. This principle has allowed capitalism to grow beyond the physical constraints of money.

19 Based on US data, the economist Richard Easterlin observed that at a point in time happiness varies directly with income both among and within nations, but over time happiness does not trend upward as income continues to grow. This is known as the Easterlin paradox. Easterlin, R. (1995). Will raising the incomes of all increase the happiness of all. *Journal of Economic Behavior and Organization, 27*(1), 35–48.

20 Kasser, T. who offers a scientific explanation of how our contemporary culture of consumerism and materialism affects our everyday happiness and psychological health. Kasser, T. (2003). *The High Price of Capitalism.* MIT Press.

21 Quoted in *New York Times*, October 14, 2019.

22 Stiglitz, J. (April 22, 2010). The non-existent hand. *London Review of Books, 32*(8), 17–18.

23 Simmons, M. R. (October 2000). www.mudcitypress.com/PDF/clubofrome.pdf.

24 Report of the World Commission on Environment and Development (also known as the Brundtland commission) (1987) *Our Common Future,* 1987.

25 United Nations. *Sustainable Development Goals.* Available at: www.un.org/sustainabledevelopment/ sustainable-development-goals/.

26 www.unglobalcompact.org.

27 Rockström et al. (2009). Planetary boundaries: Exploring the safe operating space for humanity. *Ecology and Society, 12*(2), Article 13.

28 www.stockholmresilience.org/research/research-news/2016-06-14-how-food-connects-all-the-sdgs.html. www.stockholmresilience.org/research/research-news/2016-06-14-the-sdgs-wedding-cake.html.

29 PricewaterhouseCoopers (PwC), 2015. Make it your business: Engaging with the Sustainable Development Goals. Available at: www.pwc.com/gx/en/sustainability/SDG/SDG%20Research_FINAL.pdf; BSDC 2017 report.

30 UNGC – Accenture Strategy (2019) CEO Study on Sustainability. Retrieved from www.accenture.com/tw-en/insights/strategy/ungcceostudy https://www.accenture.com/us/en/insights/strategy/ungcceostudy?c=acn_glb_purposemediarelations_11036293&n=mrl_0919.

31 www2.deloitte.com/nl/nl/pages/risk/articles/new-eu-corporate-sustainability-reporting-directive.html.

32 www.follow-this.org/nieuws/.

33 www.accenture.com/_acnmedia/PDF-134/Accenture-COVID-19-Pulse-Survey-Wave7. See also: www.bbc.com/news/business-55630144.

34 www.change.org/p/burger-king-mcd-s-save-the-environment-stop-giving-plastic-toys-with-fast-food-kids-meals.

35 Institute for Supply Chain Management November 10, 2020. Retrieved from www.ismworld.org).

36 Bales, K. (2012). *Disposable People: New Slavery in the Global Economy,* University of California Press.

37 Report by Ferry, K. May 2, 2018. Retrieved from: https://ir.kornferry.com/news-releases/news-release-details/korn-ferry-study-reveals-global-talent-shortage-could-threaten.

38 LinkedIn Report "Search of Global Talent" 2016–2019. Retrieved from https://news.linkedin.com/2019/January/linkedin-releases-2019-global-talent-trends-report.

39 Study by Deloitte. See www2.deloitte.com/global/en/pages/about-deloitte/articles/millennialsurvey.html.

40 www.theguardian.com/environment/2019/oct/13/firms-ignoring-climate-crisis-bankrupt-mark-carney-bank-england-governor.

41 Donaldson, T., & Walsh, J. P. (2015). Toward a theory of business. *Research in Organizational Behavior, 35*, 181–207.

42 Edelman Trust Barometer 2019.

Chapter 2

The Growth Triangle

The outdated value creation model

In this chapter we will explore the current dominant value creation paradigm, which we define as the Growth Triangle. Because of its outdated underlying assumptions, the model no longer serves us in these complex times. Virtually no successful, forward-looking leader (in business or government) will be using this model from 2025 onwards.

We are moving to a new paradigm, where sustainability is viewed as the value driver for business. Recognizing the interconnectedness of people, business and society, sustainability will no longer serve at the periphery, but at the center of business strategy and operations.

This is not something to consider as an "add-on", but as a whole new blueprint for the future of business. We will conclude by defining this new approach as Triple Value creation – creating value for your business, your clients and society.

For this approach to work, we will need to cultivate a "systems mindset", so that we can handle the complex, systemic and relational nature of our world. The system mindset will need to be applied at three different yet related levels: the overall economic system (System), business organization (Organization) and business leaders (Self) – which we define as SOS.

The dominant value creation paradigm of business

In classical business thinking, the purpose of business – in essence – is commonly understood to achieve financial results. How? By offering products that serve the needs of customers. The business produces and customer consumes.[1]

DOI: 10.4324/9781003119302-4

This process is enabled by capital investments. Capital is invested not only in business production assets, such as factories, digital infrastructures, brand images, logistics, research and development, but also in the purchasing power of consumers by providing loans, debts, credit cards, mortgages etc.

In this worldview, there are mainly three stakeholder groups interacting with each other: *customers* (and/or *consumers*), who have a certain demand, *producers*, who deliver the supply and *investors/shareholders*, who facilitate this process with capital. They meet at the marketplace and engage in transactions in order to realize financial value. Financial value is realized when the exchange of a good or service takes place against a profit.

It is important to note that these transactions take place against an "assumed" background of the availability of natural resources, capital and labor (the classical economic "production factors"). Also assumed is the unlimited human appetite for consumption.

Because of these assumptions, we have come to believe that business creates value by *taking, making* and *disposing* at lower cost than you sell and by increasing the number of transactions (or its margins), enabling a larger return to investors of capital.

The cycle of *capital investment–production–consumption*, which is supposed to grow year by year to increase financial value available for reinvestment in the cycle, is the dominant value creation paradigm of business today. This sounds both abstract and innocent, yet is this very paradigm that brought us to the verge of ecological collapse and unprecedented societal inequality.

That's why we want to show this belief system in a simple image, which we call the "Growth Triangle". It can be visualized in Figure 2.1.

While this model is, of course, a simplified version of what is really going on, it represents the dominant value creation paradigm of business today and – we would argue – for free-market capitalism as a whole. In fact, because of its simplified logic, it has given rise to a business culture that is preoccupied with achieving shareholder value and financial growth. The model's simplicity has been its power.

Obviously, there is nothing in nature that can grow forever. For many decades, we assumed that the Growth Triangle worked well, as its environmental effects

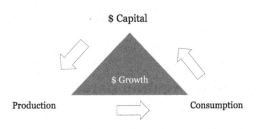

Figure 2.1 The Growth Triangle: Dominant value creation model

were delayed; now we are reaching its expiry date. If humanity is to survive on this planet, we have to redefine what we mean with growth and refine our economic paradigm. Assuming that we have infinite resources and infinite environmental capacity to absorb waste makes the economic growth model problematic and unsustainable – this could be called "narrow" or "outmoded" forms of economic growth.

Ray Anderson, founder and former CEO of Interface, one of the first sustainability business pioneers, said:

> There is the flawed view that assumes this world is ours to conquer and rule, that we can take what we want from it without regard for all the other species that depend on nature itself. The same natural world that we depend on and are part of, too. The problem is the gap between what we have and what we want; not need.[2]

Hitting a ceiling – why CSR is not enough

The first calls for sustainable development came in 1970s from concerned environmentalists who were typically projecting a somewhat "romantic" vision of sustainability as a desired utopian end state. As companies were perceived to be the major threat to reaching this desired state, business reacted rather defensively to the notion of sustainable development. But after a series of high-profile scandals in the 1990s,[3] it became usage of companies to accept "Corporate Social Responsibility" (CSR) policies as a way of ensuring a societal "license to operate". They wanted to be seen as the good guys rather than the bad guys. In the years that followed, many companies started to take measures to minimize their footprint on society and the environment. However, even though many CSR initiatives were well intended, they were ultimately understood as a tactical or operational move rather than a necessary adjustment of the business strategy and its impact on markets. CSR was typically not integrated into the core strategy. Moreover, CSR was considered a cost item – it did not alter the company's approach to value creation.

As a result, many companies ended up with a dual (and therefore confused) strategy: on the one hand, there is business as usual, and on the other, there is a CSR policy promoting something else, namely responsible business. As a result, the CSR officers found themselves in conflict with the line managers in business. The CSR managers typically managed the challenges arising from external stakeholders such as civil society, NGOs and regulators, while line managers were handling the market and customers. Overall, this created a divided leadership team, which found itself confronted with increasing amounts of conflicting objectives and trade-offs.

A very visible and painful example of how confused objectives can lead to a dramatic breach in ethics (and subsequent loss in reputation and business value) is the Dieselgate scandal of Volkswagen (see box).

Organization: Volkswagen

Volkswagen presented itself as concerned about society/environment and boasted several (CSR) initiatives in this space. But an *emissions scandal*, also known as *Dieselgate*, erupted in 2015. The United States Environmental Protection Agency found that Volkswagen had deliberately installed software in diesel engines to activate their emissions of nitrogen oxide (NOx) controls only during laboratory testing, but emit up to 40 times more NOx in real-world driving. NOx is considered a major greenhouse gas, which negatively impacts both our climate and health. In other words, Volkswagen cars poisoned the planet by emitting 40 times the legal limit of nitrogen oxide, yet the company was consciously hiding this truth from regulators. The scope of this scandal was huge: Volkswagen installed this software in about 11 million cars worldwide.

Volkswagen Group CEO Martin Winterkorn, after first denying any mistake, resigned as CEO soon after. Volkswagen was forced to announce plans to spend €16.2 billion (US$ 18.32 billion) on rectifying the emissions problems. In January 2017, Volkswagen pleaded guilty to criminal charges, and a US federal judge ordered Volkswagen to pay a $2.8 billion criminal fine for "rigging diesel-powered vehicles to cheat on government emissions tests". Later, Winterkorn was charged by prosecutors with fraud and conspiracy in the United States and Germany.[4]

The Volkswagen case is a prime example of greenwashing and the failure of CSR. The company deliberately decided to circumvent emissions control – a strategy that was known at the highest levels in the company – with the aim of giving the company a competitive advantage to remain the world's number one carmaker, by claiming that it was producing environmentally responsible cars. In the meantime, the company knew that it was poisoning our air and damaging our health and climate.[5]

The fundamental problem with CSR is that it still assumes that business and society are separate domains.

Sustainability as new business "megatrend"

What lies beyond the CSR approach? More and more companies started to recognize that the new reality of interdependence between business and society is the next business "megatrend", just like IT, Globalization and the Internet did earlier. Such megatrends determine the long-term viability of a business. Playing on the words of Milton Friedman, management scholar Frank Horwitz appropriately states: "The only business of business now is *sustainable business*"[6]. This is to say: "business as usual" – without heed to the wider setting – is no longer an option. We now need to rewrite the narrative that is underlying business.

An indication of this change of heart in business leadership is the statement made by the Business Roundtable, an association of major US-based companies, in September 2019, with the aim to redefine a corporation's purpose. The statement, which was signed by 181 of the group's 188 member CEOs, said that "whereas creating shareholder value was once the main objective of American businesses, this goal should be changed to delivering value to all constituencies, from customers to the world at large".[7]

The language used represents a major shift in how leading CEOs have defined the roles in public: for decades they publicly promoted shareholder value primacy, but now their words acknowledge that business interests cannot be separated from the interests of society.

This clearly demonstrates the "Beyond CSR" viewpoint: by definition, as business cannot survive without society, the interests of society are of a higher order than the interests of companies. Businesses are embedded in society, rather than that business should do good just for business. The following illustration shows where the disconnect is taking place, and what needs to be done to expand the scope of awareness and concern: from serving markets only to serving markets, societies and ecosystems.

In order to solve the disconnect between business and society/planet, companies need to become aware that they are dependent upon healthy societies and

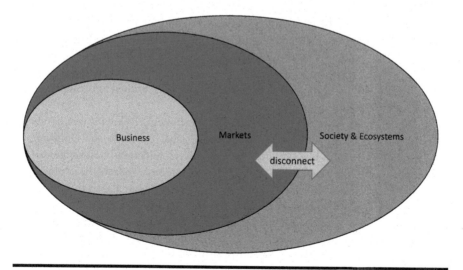

Figure 2.2 Disconnect

ecosystems. It is a reality in which the needs of organizations, customers, markets, society and ecosystem are dependent upon each other and equally important. This is essentially an "outside-in" *perspective* (which we will also define as the "systems perspective") looking from the larger outer context inward to the core of business, its value creation principles and its purpose.

In contrast, the CSR approach was based on an "inside-out" perspective in which it recognized that the company has some responsibility for society and nature, but not so far as to see that nature and society are the very fundaments of a healthy, future-fit and flourishing organization. This inside-out CSR approach no longer serves us now that the outer context is crashing onto our doorsteps.

Most significantly, we need to recognize that the contextual changes are disrupting the current value creation models of companies. This is the central theme in this book, and will lead us into recognizing how the challenges in the context can be "flipped" into business opportunities. In order to embrace *the outside-in perspective*, business leaders will need to become capable of aligning and engaging deeply with the interests of multiple stakeholders, understanding the root causes of disruption, and seeing both the short and long term. They will need to understand how they and their business can contribute to solving the most pressing societal and environmental challenges that they strategically relate to and depend upon.

A company demonstrating this transition is Unilever, the Anglo-Dutch giant in fast-moving consumer goods, which has evolved into the globally most recognized sustainable company.[8]

Organization: Unilever case study

The Unilever brand will not be known to everyone, but if you ever washed with a Dove soap, enjoyed a cup of Lipton tea, eaten a tub of Ben & Jerry's ice cream, took a bite of Lay's potato crisp or styled your hair with Toni & Guy, you have been in touch with the firm.

In 2011, Unilever announced the Sustainable Living Plan (SLP) in an effort to build its entire business on serving societal and sustainability goals. Paul Polman, CEO from 2008 until 2019, became personified as the leader of business sustainability.[9]

When he commenced his CEO role, Polman spoke the following words: "As a leader I am NOT guided by the question: what can I do for Unilever? My question is: what can Unilever do for society? And then I ask: how can I support Unilever to fulfill that mission?" This statement reflects that Polman put his leadership not only at the service of his company but also at the service of sustainability. This represented the next level in the firm's leadership.

Polman's ambition culminated in the SLP, which set a number of bold goals: (1) to improve the health and well-being of more than one billion with their personal care, hygiene and nutritional brands and business; (2) to reduce the environmental footprint and negative impact of the production and use their products by half in 2030 and (3) to enhance the livelihoods of millions of people focusing on opportunities for woman, inclusive business and smallholders. At the same time, Unilever set out to double its business revenue. Jeff Seabright, chief sustainability officer at Unilever at that time, said the SLP was not so much a sustainability plan but a *sustainable business plan*. "Sustainable business drives superior performance and is the only way to create long-term value for all their stakeholders", he said.[10]

When Paul Polman was appointed as the representative of the global business community at the negotiations for the UN Sustainable Development Goals (SDGs), he made sure that Unilever's SLP objectives became fully aligned to the SDGs. He also created clear measurable benchmarks for these goals and linked those to executive performance compensation.

The results have been impressive: its peers regard Unilever as the most sustainable company. According to a 2018 survey,[11] the SLP has made Unilever a key talent attractor with 75% of employees believing their role contributes to the SLP and 70% believing they can fulfill their purpose at work. In addition, 92% of employees who believe they can be true to their purpose at Unilever, also say that their job inspires them to give themselves fully to their work. In 2018, Unilever topped the list of preferred employers among graduates of leading business schools from where the firm recruits its future employees.

And all this drove the financial performance of the firm: after ten years the total shareholder return has been 290%, while over €1 billion cost were avoided and the supply chain has become increasingly future-proof against climate change and other risks.[12]

Beyond CSR: sustainability as value creation

The Unilever case illustrates how a company progresses through a number of stages, gradually expanding the perspective on society and increasing its sustainability ambitions. It entails a shift from the *inside-out approach* of CSR to the *outside-in approach* of viewing sustainability from the viewpoint of strategic growth. Paul Polman described this stage as "turning CSR into SRC: becoming a Social Responsible Company".[13]

Another example of such "beyond CSR approach" is Microsoft, when CEO Satya Nadella announced in 2019 an ambitious commitment: to become carbon negative by 2030 and remove more carbon than they directly emitted since their founding from the environment by 2050. "No one company can solve this macro challenge alone, but as a global technology company we have a particular responsibility to do our part", Satya Nadella said. Since the announcement, Microsoft has

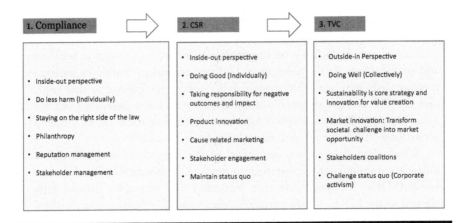

Figure 2.3 Stages in corporate sustainability

added commitments to become water positive, zero waste and to protect more land than we use by 2030.[14] Especially the commitment to remove from the environment all the carbon the company has emitted (either directly or by electrical consumption) since it was founded in 1975 is a remarkable step in complex sustainability leadership. No firm of the size of Microsoft has voluntarily made such a retrospective footprint commitment.

In particular, the Unilever and Microsoft examples illustrate that sustainability can be merged with the strategy of the firm. Sustainability is no longer on the periphery of the firm, but at the center. It enables the company to *create sustainable value* by serving the needs of consumers and society in an integrated manner. A significant feature of this stage is that the company is discovering its *shared purpose* with society. In fact, at this stage the company leadership realizes that its shareholder value creation process is *dependent* on its ability to create societal value. There is no longer any conflict between the two.

There is another dimension that these front-running companies demonstrate: sustainability is a major source of inspiration for one's employees, investors and consumers. It is an attractor for new talent, while it drives the latest stage of evolution in business sustainability. Somehow this next stage beyond CSR represents a "win-win" for all stakeholders.

We define this next stage as *Triple Value creation* (TVC): the company starts to create value for society, its clients and its own organization simultaneously, without unnecessary trade-offs. In this definition, society includes the environment, which is the highest order of systems that we depend on. Alan Jope, current CEO of Unilever, recognizes this integrated approach: "The future of business should be based on values of humanity and empathy. Simply because our employees demand it, our clients expect it and the planet needs it".[15] This will be discussed in detail in Chapters 5 and 6.

Bringing together the various elements of business sustainability that evolved over the last years, we can now conceive of the trajectory of three stages from Compliance, CSR to TVC. The last step – from CSR to TVC – is a big yet necessary shift we are now facing as a collective: companies have to move from "individually doing good" to "collectively doing well". Although this may seem difficult, the upside is tremendous: business will be able to unleash the shared purpose between its people, its clients and society, thereby upgrading their "license to operate" to a "license to flourish".

This does not necessarily mean that all firms transition linearly from one stage to the other – a company such as Tesla seems to have started largely at the CSR/TVC level, for example. Nor do the stages have neatly discernable features. But the stage model can help companies to know where they are and how they can move forward.

What next? Toward a "systems view"

As we have seen, a leader, an organization or a country, for that matter, cannot solve the challenges facing business in isolation. Climate, energy, migration, health, inequality, biodiversity and poverty – these are all interdependent and interrelated, and they impact business in multiple and unpredictable ways. The way to tackle them requires a *systems view*, which means that we have to look at the context, relationships and patterns that have given rise to these problems instead of looking at one problem at a time.

This is critical for the business leadership of the future; it needs to employ a *systems mindset* that can generate systemic solutions for the challenges of clients and society.

As the examples of Unilever and Microsoft show (and we will show more examples throughout this book), there is a way to develop such a systems mindset and cater for the multiple needs of customers and society simultaneously. This is the only way that companies can create sustainable value in the complex world of today and become part of the solution rather than the problem.

The systems mindset that recognizes the relational and interdependent nature of complex challenges is an advanced stage of development for both leaders and their organizations. This book is devoted to making this mindset accessible for leaders.

At the root of this work is the belief that we as human beings have the potential to change. We are not mindless machines – we are living creatures who have the capacity to feel, relate, reflect and create. Most importantly, we can be aware. We can be aware of our context and ourselves.

This is a unique part of human nature – the capacity to *become aware* of the effects of our actions and, on this basis, change the way we think and act. This means that, as a matter of principle, we have the capacity to develop a systems view of the dynamic world around us and adapt ourselves accordingly.

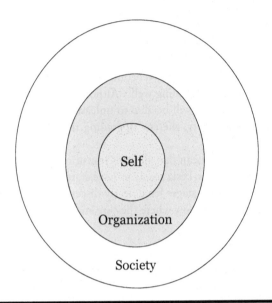

Figure 2.4 SOS model

Three interrelated levels of complexity

In fact, in our research we have found that we need change at three levels of complexity: new macroeconomic models, new business models and a new leadership compass. Just changing one of these levels will not be enough. Just changing laws and financial incentives won't do it. We will also need to change the purpose and structure of organizations. But this won't do the trick if we don't upgrade our way of thinking – especially the mindset and beliefs of the leaders. Leaders are working at the edge of the systems shift – they feel the brunt of clashing worldviews. Systems change starts with leadership.

This is well summed up by Feike Sybesma, former CEO of Royal DSM: "How can you be successful as a leader, if your organization is not successful? How can you be successful as an organization, if the society in which it operates is not successful?"[16]

We can summarize these three levels as Systems, Organizations and Self, with the acronym SOS, which is an appropriate reminder of the sense of urgency that is required for the transformation of our current systems.

We will interweave these three levels of complexity into the narrative of this book, illustrated by "boxes" that describe the background of larger systems insights ("System"), example of business case studies ("Organization") and leadership reflections and examples. ("Self / Leadership"). We will also add relevant insights from science ("Science").

In Chapter 3, we will explore the paradigm shift that is occurring in science. While economics and business has modeled itself on physics, we will see that the new life science, biology and psychology, in particular, have moved forward and presented a new framework on which we can organize our economic activity. The new science in fact reveals a powerful *systems perspective* that business leadership is looking for to deal with today's systems challenge. This perspective, in turn, will help us to conceive of a new more sustainable value creation model and the leadership practices to realize them.

As system thinking expert Donella Meadows affirms:

> We humans are smart enough to have created complex systems and amazing productivity; surely we are also smart enough to make sure that everyone shares our bounty, and surely we are smart enough to sustainably steward the natural world upon which we all depend.[17]

Notes

1 This is the classical logic, but it excludes manufactured demand, which emerged much later. For example, consumers may readily buy bottled water imported all the way from the Fiji islands, but do they really need it or is the demand manufactured through marketing?

2 Harel, T., Van Arkel, G., Van Der Pluijm, F., & Aanraad, B. *Interface, The Journey of a Lifetime,* The Natural Step (2013).

3 Examples are Royal Dutch Shell oil company, which decided to sink the Brent Spar oil platform in the North Sea and the discovery that sportswear firm Nike which was using sweat shops in Asia for the production of their running shoes.

4 www.techtimes.com/articles/2017-01-10/volkswagen-executive-arrested-over-dieselgate-scandal.htm.

5 Ibidem.

6 Horwitz, F. M., & Grayson, D. (2010). Putting sustainability into practice in a business school. *Global Focus,* 4(2), 26–29.

7 September 2019. www.businessroundtable.org/business-roundtable-redefines-the-purpose-of-a-corporation-to-promote-an-economy-that-serves-all-americans.

8 For the tenth year in a row, Unilever is regarded as the number one corporate sustainability leader, with expert respondents identifying the company as a "leader in integrating sustainability into its business strategy"; https://globescan.com/unilever-patagonia-ikea-interface-top-sustainability-leaders-2020/.

9 www.reutersevents.com/sustainability/farewell-paul-polman-epitome-twenty-first-century-ceo.

10 Private interview.

11 UniVoice Survey 2018 – www.unilever.com.

12 www.unilever.com/investor-relations/annual-report-and-accounts/.

13 Polman, P., & Winston, A. (2021). *The Net Positive Manifesto,* Harvard Business Review.

14 Joppa, L. Chief Environmental Officer of Microsoft. *This is bigger than all of us: why Microsoft is signing The Climate Pledge.* Published in LinkedIn on December 9, 2020.

15 Jope, A. Interview in Unilever Future Leaders League. (2020). www.facebook.com/watch/?v=291511848695433.

16 Interview webinar March 28, 2020.

17 https://donellameadows.org/about-donella-meadows/.

Chapter 3

The paradigm shift in science

The living systems view

In this chapter we will explore the paradigm shift that is taking place in science. (As this chapter contains a lot of abstract theory, the reader who is merely interested in practical business issues may want to skip this chapter.)

We will describe how we are moving away from the material worldview that underpinned classical economics and business to a new paradigm suggesting that all social phenomena – including economies and business – are subject to principles shared by *living systems*. In the new paradigm, emphasis is given to complexity, networks and patterns of organization, with the aim of creating generative and sustainable systems.

In terms of organizations, this means that we have to shift from the metaphor of a "mindless non-linear machine" to that of a "mindful complex adaptive system". The health and vitality of complex adaptive systems is determined by six key principles – the *six principles of life*.

We will see that such systems do not strive for optimal efficiency, as the machine metaphor suggests. Instead, healthy and sustainable systems are striving for optimal balance between efficiency and resilience, based on connectivity, diversity and redundancy.

This will provide a fundamental and radical shift in perspective on business. It will enable leaders to align their organizations and policies to those forces that unleash flow and vitality for the system as a whole and its constituent members.

DOI: 10.4324/9781003119302-5

The paradigm that drives the Growth Triangle

The Growth Triangle model, which simplified value creation as an arrangement between producers, consumers and investors, evolved from ideas in the scientific revolution more than 200 years ago. Today, however, this simple model is no longer effective in the face of the complex sustainability challenges, as we described in Chapter 1. The paradigm has changed. That's why business as usual doesn't work anymore.

As the great 20th century economist John Maynard Keynes observed, beliefs matter. He wrote, "The ideas of economists and political philosophers, both when they are right and when they are wrong, are more powerful than is commonly understood. Indeed, the world is ruled by little else".

Beliefs are assumptions we hold to be true, individually and collectively – and in time these can become unconscious beliefs or a paradigm. Thomas Kuhn, who studied the evolution in scientific thinking over centuries, defined *paradigm* as "a comprehensive model of understanding that provides a field's members with viewpoints and rules on how to look at the field's problems and how to solve them".[1] In other words, paradigms determine how we understand reality, and on the basis of that understanding, navigate and make meaning of the world.

An example of a paradigm is the belief that the "world is flat", which was a common view until just a few centuries ago. Nowadays, we all believe the "the earth is round", so the old paradigm has been replaced by a new paradigm. This paradigm may change further in the future (in reality, the earth is an oblate ellipsoid with the continents slowly creeping around the surface). When paradigms are not adjusted in response to a changing reality, they can become problematic. They can become static, rigid and self-serving. This will prevent us from seeing new emerging realities and make meaning of the changes that are coming, withholding us from taking appropriate action in response to these changes.

This paradigm shift is now also apparent in business and economics. As management thinker Gary Hamel expressed:

> The biggest barrier to the transformation of capitalism cannot be found within the observable realm of org charts, strategic plans and quarterly reports, but rather within the human mind itself [...]. The true enemy of our times is a matrix of deeply held beliefs about what business is actually for, who it serves and how it creates value.[2]

So let's explore the origins of the current predominant paradigm.

The material worldview

Inspired by the scientific revolution driven by breakthrough insights in physics and chemistry, the early economists sought to establish economics as a natural science, just like physics and chemistry. The founder of modern physics, Isaac Newton, in 1687, perceived the universe to consist of isolated atoms interacting which each other through "mechanical laws" with predictable outcomes.[3] This gave rise to the "material worldview" – all things are merely physical objects, operating more or less independently from each other and to be understood linearly and mechanistically. In doing so, Newton validated a stream of thought that goes back to the early history of philosophy in ancient Greece. Democritus described the universe as a big empty space in which isolated atoms move on the basis *physical material laws*, regardless of human actions. When Euclid developed a mathematical model to capture these laws, the idea of a measurable and predictable universe arose.

There were many other philosophies at that time. For example, Plato contrasted the material views with a more mystical understanding of life, in which there was room for *Telos* – invariably translated as "life force" or "purpose" – that permeates the material dimension of life and provides a role for cognition and meaning for human beings.[4] In fact, the Catholic Church absorbed many of the Platonic ideals of a mystical, conscious and creative universe. Nonetheless, with the advent of modern science in the 17th century, Newtonian physics – and economics in its slipstream – adopted the material and mechanical view of a lifeless universe, with a reductionist approach to understanding reality. This has been the dominant scientific paradigm up to very recently, which has greatly influenced our thinking on economics and business.

Science: Machine metaphor for management

In 17th century Europe, a metaphor of "nature as a machine" took hold and became so ingrained that today we have forgotten that it is a metaphor. In the theory of scientific management, formulated in 1903 by economist Frederick Taylor, the idea was to model business on the image of a machine, designed to create evergrowing output of products and services to be sold to consumers acting mainly for their own interest.[5] Thus business management should act as chief engineer, making sure the machine runs efficiently. Capital is the fuel used to fire up the engine of productivity. The larger context of society is not relevant – the role of companies is limited to working along the invisible hand of the market.

These ideas are also known as Taylorism, after its founder, which influence is still felt today.[6] Many economists and management thinkers implicitly assume it's their job to make sure our economies and companies function as efficient profit-making machines. In the machine model the top-leadership is supposed to be of extraordinary intelligence, just like the top-engineer who controls the machine. All business functions, such as marketing, finance, HR and supply chain management, can be executed and controlled by experts in their respective fields.

> While this machine-like metaphor has helped industrial firms to grow and go to scale, it had a serious by-effect: management has lost the understanding of *the systemic way* that an organization creates value.

Increasingly, business scholars and practitioners have been challenging this paradigm. Former Shell executive Arie De Geus, in his classic *The Living Company*, argues for going beyond the material paradigm by applying principles of biology and psychology to the way we run companies. Having studied the longevity of organizations, he concludes: "the most enduring companies treat their enterprises as 'living work communities' rather than purely economic machines".[7]

Contemporary economist Tim Jackson echoes this view on a systems level:

> It is time we transcend the credo of capitalism. Capitalism is so entrenched in materialism that it ignores the possibility for human and social flourishing. Capitalism assumes that the purpose of human life is to produce and consume material goods, failing to see the richness and diversity that human life has available and ready for cultivation towards a state of flow and well-being.[8]

The systems view of life

As said, classical economics and business thinking have modeled themselves on the Newtonian logic of determinism, reductionism and predictability, assuming that economies are material phenomena. Advances in academic thinking have indicated that this assumption is flawed: economics and business studies are now generally understood to be social sciences, as they study human behavior.[9]

As such, they should incorporate findings from biology, sociology, psychology and complexity sciences, amongst others. The emerging consensus is that economic entities do not behave as "machines" but as "living systems".[10]

Living systems comprise different functions than nonliving systems – they behave differently. Indeed, living systems – also technically known as complex adaptive systems[11] – have a dual nature: *material* (such as a form or structure) and *immaterial* (such as a dynamic pattern or relationship). In contrast to the material paradigm, which assumes that the world consists *merely* of matter, the living systems view recognizes both the material and immaterial dimension. In fact, the living systems view realizes that it is the immaterial *patterns and relationships* that fundamentally shape our world, including the material structures. As biologist Francisco Varela writes: "This world is our dance together – not my projection, not yours. It's something we do together, and what we do changes what the world is like".[12]

To translate this into business terms, rather than assuming that companies are *merely material* entities with legal status, assets and production capacity designed for efficiency, the new insight is that companies are primarily dynamic networks of interactive human beings with *immaterial* (or "living") qualities. In fact, it is because of these living qualities that organizations create value and human societies flourish.

Economic philosopher Jeremy Lent explains:

> Far from being separate from the rest of nature, we are part of an endless meshwork of life going back over billions of years. And as humans evolved into a unique species, cooperation was their defining characteristic. Alone among primates, we developed moral emotions – such as compassion, shame, and a visceral sense of fairness – that caused our identity to expand beyond individual selves and incorporate our entire group.[13]

More than two decades after Arie de Geus published the Living Company, there is overwhelming evidence to conclude that organizations can only be properly managed and steered toward value creation when we consider these living qualities.[14] What does this mean in the practice of business?

Six patterns of self-organization

Biologists have observed that all types of organisms are capable of reproduction, renewal, growth and development, connection, maintenance and response to stimuli.[15] The endless complexity of life is organized into patterns of behavior that tend to repeat themselves. All nature is a continuum.

The chemist and Nobel Prize Laureates Illya Prigogine proposed that living systems are run on the principle of "Self-organization".[16] In a self-organizing system – unlike a machine – there is no central factor or predesign driving the system, but an emerging pattern of self-organization involving all parts of the system.

We can identify roughly six dominant patterns that signify a healthy organism. On the basis of these insights, we have identified **the six key principles** that operate in all living systems, which can be utilized by leadership to create healthy and sustainable business systems. While they are derived from biology and systems science, they correspond to the latest insights from cognitive science – hence we will use terms from these disciplines to describe them.[17] We will call these the six principles of life.

Six principles of life

Context-relatedness: Systems view

Living systems are open systems with input and output flows, consisting of matter, energy or information in exchange with their context. This makes them different from nonliving matter. These flows are usually facilitated by a membrane, which separates the organism from the external environment. The membrane has a selectively permeable function, through which its sets and maintains boundaries and keeps the system integrated within a changing context. In psychological terms, the ability to relate to the context can be described as the "systems view". It corresponds to the ability to deal with complexity and a state of psychological integration.

Consciousness: Learning and adaptation

Living systems are cognitive systems. Modern biology affirms that this statement is valid for all organisms, with or without nervous systems.[18] Cognition co-emerges with the interaction between the system and its environment. When the organism faces challenges or problems from the environment, it uses cognition or consciousness (which includes memory) to come up with a solution. Consciousness drives a process of continuous learning, with as outcome successful adaptation.[19]

Centeredness: Homeostasis

While the organism is constantly changing, renewing and adapting, there is a process of maintenance occurring as well – it wants to preserve its core or center. Homeostasis refers to the maintenance within a living system to bounce back from disruptive changes and restore the system to a state of equilibrium. In terms of psychology, we speak of mission, values and culture to describe the same pattern of preserving the core.

Connectedness: Symbiosis

Living systems are constantly engaged in symbiotic relationships. Symbiosis is a close and sustaining biological interaction between two different biological organisms. A symbiosis occurs when there is mutual benefit to each partner. As human beings evolved into a unique species, cooperation and collaboration are their defining characteristics. This pattern constitutes the connectivity that living systems need. In psychology, we speak of relatedness as well as the qualities of care and compassion.

Competence: Efficiency

Competence is the ability to do something efficiently by streamlining its activities. For organisms to survive, they will need to be competent in obtaining resources such as food, water or territory in limited supply, or for access to mates for reproduction. This may involve a sense of competition with other species. Yet while a degree of competition is natural for species, this is often a temporary state within a larger ecosystem with mutually beneficial symbiosis between species, enhancing the overall resilience of the ecosystem.

Creativity: Regeneration

Living systems are never static; they constantly change and renew themselves, which facilitates a process of evolution in organisms over time across generations. This process of regeneration allows organisms to evolve into the diversity that is needed for the health of the ecosystem. Regeneration implies that the species is truly adaptable and sustainable in a changing context. In psychology terms, all this corresponds to qualities of adaptation, creativity and innovation.

Striving for optimal balance

Let's consider why these insights from the systems view of life are so different from the material paradigm that we know so well in business today.

System scientists determined that when these six principles are fully activated and well balanced, there are **two outcomes** that determine the living system's vitality and sustainability: *efficiency* on the one hand and *resilience* on the other.[20] Efficiency is the ability of the system to absorb quantities of energy of information. Resilience allows the system to rebalance and renew itself after an external force has disturbed it.

Resilience of a system is enhanced by redundancy, diversity and connectivity. Redundancy refers to access capacity provided by homeostasis, diversity refers to the various parts of the system that serve as coordinating nodes in the network, while connectivity refers to the pathways connecting the nodes. Importantly, connectivity extends both inside and outside the organization, forming an integrated ecosystem with its surroundings.

Efficiency is achieved by the *streamlining* of the system. Streamlining requires redundancy/homeostasis, diversity and connectivity to be reduced. This can only be done for a short time, until the system starts to react.

This is *the crux of living systems science*: living systems don't have a natural drive to achieve optimal efficiency. If they would extend this drive toward efficiency, they would comprise their resilience – they would die. What they do to strive for is the *optimal balance* between efficiency and resilience. Both of these forces are indispensable for the health and vitality of any living system and its regenerative capacity over time.

Any pressure on account of either efficiency or resilience will lead to the malfunctioning of the system. Too much emphasis on efficiency can lead to a structural in or explosion, while too much emphasis on resilience will lead to inertia and stagnation.

In short, the sustainability of a complex system can be defined as the *optimal balance between efficiency and resilience*. They can be seen in Figure 3.1.

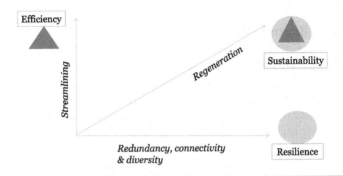

Figure 3.1 Efficiency and resilience = sustainability

Science: Efficiency and resilience in anthropology

Bruce Gibb, an anthropologist of the University of Michigan, researched the factors that had led to the demise and survival of Native American tribes.[21] Looking at which tribes survived to the present day, and which tribes disappeared as viable living communities, he discovered that healthy tribes maintained a dual pattern of leadership.

When tribes are busy working on the fields or hunting, or when they have to defend their territories against intruders, they organize themselves into highly efficient structures, with centralized leadership. Any sense of divergence is "streamlined" on the way.

However, when the tribe is at rest and peace, they demonstrate a very different organizational structure, with a non-centralized shared leadership style – it's all about diversity and connectivity. All community members are engaged in rituals around the campfire, with the full participation of all members, young and old. There is no central leadership at these community events. At times of peace, they would also exchange and connect with other tribes and form alliances.

Tribes and civilizations that maintain the leadership to alternate between these styles of organization – ensuring efficiency and resilience respectively and retain connectedness with the larger ecosystem – have been able to survive and evolve over time, adapting to the changes in the context. Both styles are needed; if one would be neglected, the tribe could become isolated or disintegrate.

The efficiency trade-off

These insights from system science can help explain why our current economic model has become so unstable and "out of flow": the Triangle of Growth is designed to create optimal efficiency of invested capital and production, while ignoring the health of the systems of which it is a part. If business as one subset of a system drives efficiency, it will gradually undermine the vitality and health of the entire system.

Echoing the words of the complexity scientists is Harvard economist Roger L. Martin, who wrote in a book advising CEOs about performance, "Resilient systems are typically characterized by the very features – diversity and redundancy, or slack – that efficiency seeks to destroy".[22] He continues: "We pushed the pursuit of efficiency to such an obsessive level, creating massive wealth for those at the top while ignoring the needs at the bottom, yet it is this very inequality that undermines the functioning of the economy".

We have seen these principles at play with monoculture farming techniques. For example, the reliance on Cavendish bananas might have been very cost-efficient, yet the clack of variation has made the crops highly susceptible to disease.[23] Likewise, today's large-scale, specialized and centralized supply chains are highly efficient and cost-effective, but their corresponding lack of redundancy, diversity and interconnectivity makes it rigid and highly susceptible to failure when confronted with an unexpected challenge. The system may be highly optimized with minimum redundancy, yet the lack of buffers will diminish its chances for recovery.

The same applies to the way we organize our companies. When the sole purpose of corporations is to maximize shareholder returns by optimized efficiency, a dangerous feedback loop is created where short-term financial successes come at the expense of long-term resilience. Marc Benioff, CEO of Salesforce, expresses this insight in words: "Excessive focus on creating shareholder value goes at the expense of creating stakeholder value. A healthy company needs to balance these objectives, like two hands working together".[24]

The new integrated perspective

More than two centuries after Isaac Newton, we can conclude that the material and mechanical beliefs embedded in our current business paradigm fail to provide the *systems view* that is needed for dealing effectively with multifaceted challenge of sustainability. The old beliefs resting on reductionism, efficiency and specialization, which have been useful for achieving economic efficiency, are literally *too narrow* for the complex reality today. The new and undeniable reality is that people, business and society function as a *complex adaptive system*, for which economic efficiency alone is not enough to survive.

The question now is how can we discard our materialistic blindfold and recognize the more accurate perspective of living systems? Can we articulate a more holistic, relational and comprehensive view in agreement with the principles of life, in which efficiency and resilience are in balance, with a view on achieving genuine sustainability? Can we move from the Growth Triangle to the Circle of Sustainability?

Figure 3.2 The Circle of Sustainability

We propose to visualize the new and more empowering perspective in Figure 3.2. In the following chapters, we will use this comprehensive frame to explore the transition toward sustainability, applying this to the levels of systems, organizations and ourselves as leaders (SOS).

We will use these colors and symbols to guide you on the journey.

Notes

1 Kuhn, T. (1962). *The Structure of Scientific Revolutions*, Chicago, IL: University of Chicago Press.
2 Hamel, G., & Breen, B. (2007). *The Future of Management.* Cambridge, MA: Harvard Business School Publishing.
3 Newton, I. (1687). *Philosophia Naturalis Principia Mathematica. Newton, Sir Isaac (2020). The Mathematical Principles of Natural Philosophy.* London: Flame Tree Publishing.
4 Lent, J. (2017). *The Patterning Instinct. A Cultural History of Humanity's Search for Meaning.* Amherst, NY: Prometheus Books.
5 Taylor, F. W. (1903). *Shop Management,* New York, NY: American Society of Mechanical Engineers.
6 Aitken, H. G. J. (1985). *Scientific Management in Action,* Princeton, NJ: Princeton University Press.
7 De Geus, A. (1997). *The Living Company – Habits for Survival in a Turbulent Business Environment.* Boston: Harvard Business Press.
8 Jackson, T. (2021). *Post Growth – Life after Capitalism.* Cambridge, UK: Polity.
9 The classical definition of economics, as expressed by Lion Robbins in 1932, is "the science which studies human behavior as a relation between scarce means having alternative uses". Robbins, L. (1932) *Essay on the Nature and Significance of Economic Science.* London: Macmillan.
10 Capra, F., & Luigi, L. (2016). *Systems View of Life – A Unifying Vision.* Cambridge, MA: Cambridge University Press; Lent, J. (2017). *The Patterning Instinct: A Cultural History of Humanity's Search for Meaning.* Lanham, MD: Prometheos Books.
11 Holland, J.H. (1992), *Adaptation in Natural and Artificial Systems: An Introductory Analysis with Applications to Biology, Control, and Artificial Intelligence.* Cambridge, MA: MIT Press.

12 Varela, F., Rosh, E., & Thomson, E. (2017). *The Embodied Mind: Cognitive Science and Human Experience.* Cambridge, MA: MIT Press.

13 www.kosmosjournal.org/kj_article/awakening-to-life/.

14 Derived from the work of system scientists James Grier Miller, Humberto Maturana, Francesco Varela, Fritjof Capra and Luis Luigi (references in other notes in this book).

15 The living systems theory is developed by Miller, J. G. (1978). *Living Systems.* New York: McGraw-Hill. Instead of examining phenomena by attempting to break things down into components, the living systems theory explores phenomena in terms of dynamic patterns of the relationships of organisms with their environment.

16 Prigogine, I., & Nicolis, G. (1977). *Self-Organization in Non-Equilibrium Systems.* New York: Wiley.

17 Daniel, S. (2012). *Pocket Guide to Interpersonal Neurobiology: An Integrative Handbook of the Mind;* Norton Series on Interpersonal Neurobiology.

18 Maturana, H. R., & Varela, F. J. (1980). *Autopoiesis and Cognition. The Realization of the Living.* Dordrecht: Reidel, p. 13.

19 Varela, F. J., Thompson, E., & Rosch, E. (1991). *The Embodied Mind: Cognitive Science and Human Experience.* Cambridge, MA: MIT Press.

20 Ulanowicz, R. E., Goerner, S. J., Lietear, B., & Gomez, R. (2009). Quantifying sustainability. *Journal of Ecological Complexity,* 6(1), 27–36.

21 This was derived from a lecture given by Bruce Gibb at the Whole System Change summit in 2006 in Boston.

22 Martin, R. (2020). *When More Is not Better: Overcoming America's Obsession with Economic Efficiency.* Boston: Harvard Business Review Press.

23 Steavenson, W. March 3, 2021. www.prospectmagazine.co.uk/society-and-culture/battle-for-food-environment-agriculture-big-ag-climate-change-wendell-steavenson.

24 Interview of Benioff, M. Retrieved from www.youtube.com/watch?v=ohZP0zJxnG0.

Part 2

What?

What is the new approach to value creation?

Chapter 4

Toward a systems view of value creation – six shifts

In this chapter we will explore the shifts in thinking at a systems level that are taking place. By referring to the six principles of life, we will identify six main beliefs behind the dominant Growth Triangle model that are now subject to change. We will discuss each of these beliefs, indicating how they have trapped us into a pattern of behavior that drives our environmentally destructive and unsustainable business practices, and how they can be flipped into new beliefs that are more in alignment with reality and provide business with a new lens on value creation.

This approach will show that nothing is static. The ideas of a lifeless mechanical universe that worked in the past no longer suit us and are being replaced by new more inspiring and life-affirming ideas. Change is already on the way. The successful, forward-looking leaders are actively challenging the old beliefs as they move to a more sustainable and generative business paradigm more suited to the needs of today. The brightest emerging talent, all around the world, will be part of a new wave that embraces a more relational and positive vision for the role of business in society.

Six old and new beliefs

In Chapter 3, we have seen that if we want to develop a sustainable value creation model – one that creates/generates value rather than extracts/destroys value – we will have to move from the Growth Triangle to the Circle of Sustainability. If the

DOI: 10.4324/9781003119302-7

old beliefs and values of the Growth Triangle are the "enemy" of our times, then we must find the *new* beliefs and values underpinning the Circle of Sustainability that can replace the old ones.

Since – as we discussed – we have found six principles of life drive the health and vitality of all living systems, it makes sense to use these principles to identify the changes needed in our economic thinking. The six principles could be useful frames to simplify a complex process of debate that is happening in the literature on economics and business, as well as help us analyze the changes that are occurring in many leading companies as they move to sustainability.

Through this analysis, we will be able to present six new beliefs that can serve as the antithesis of six beliefs that underpin the old model. In a sense, the six new beliefs constitute a new paradigm that is more suited to drive sustainable value creation than the old beliefs. The six new beliefs are the following:

	Six C principles	Old beliefs	New beliefs
1	Context	Business and Society are separate	Business and Society are One
2	Consciousness	Homo Economicus	Homo sapiens
3	Centeredness	Nature is Free	Planetary health
4	Connection	Shareholders First	Stakeholder model
5	Competence	Markets are (self-regulatory) transactions	Markets are (generative) relationships
6	Creativity	Short-term profit	Long-term impact

Many of these beliefs have been unearthed before. The point here is to realize that these old beliefs are actually still influential in a world where the sustainability trend has reached a tipping point, but where many business leaders remain stuck in old paradigms of value destruction. We now need a deeper insight to go from lofty

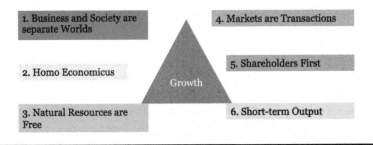

Figure 4.1 The Growth Triangle – six old beliefs

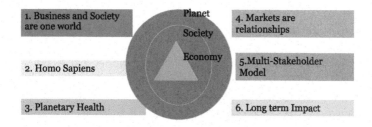

Figure 4.2 The Circle of Sustainability – six new beliefs

CSR statements (or, worse, greenwashing) to actual commitment to authentic sustainable transformation.

What follows should be taken not as a set of beliefs that somehow stands aside from day-to-day business practice. Rather, as we will go on to see, the shifts infuse the entire strategic vision for what the organization is for – and how it conducts itself in all respects.

Because the six beliefs are a simplification of a complex narrative that evolved over several centuries, we will illustrate the six beliefs with brief captions of the evolution of economic thought.

Shift 1 (Context): From "Business and Society are Separate", to "Business and Society are One"

Inspired by the material worldview and the reductionist approach from physics, the classical economists conceived the world to consist of separate components, such as public and private domains, distinguishing *public* from *private* goods. Like the laws of the natural world, these components are believed to be held together and interact with each other by "laws" such as the law of supply and demand.

Private goods are the domain of individuals and entrepreneurs who operate in competitive markets, while public goods are all those that are not private, generally falling under the categories of society and the environment. Hence, we made a distinction between the private and public sectors. In most modern democracies, we conceived of a "Social Contract" to regulate the relationship between these two sectors.

System: The Social Contract

French philosopher Jean-Jacques Rousseau, in his 1762 book "The Social Contract", states that "governments should draw their power from the governed, its 'sovereign' people, and that no person should have absolute power, and that a *legitimate* state is one which meets the needs and wishes of its citizens".[1] These include peace, security, economic development and the resolution of conflict.

The Social Contract was a reaction to the centuries' old feudal system, in which individuals were often subject to the whims of greedy landlords or power-hungry clergy. The idea was to find a new justification for government by limiting the divine rights of priests and kings. In exchange, individuals were asked to relinquish some of their natural rights in order for the state to provide social order by the rule of law. This revolutionary idea formed the basis for modern democracy.

The key principle underlying the Social Contract is that the state recognizes human rights. Importantly, this principle implied that the state also recognizes private property rights. European nations adopted principles from Roman law to define these rights. The Latin term "*privatus*" means "to set apart, belonging to oneself (not to the state)", set in contrast to *publicus*, or community. Thus, private property originated as an important element of the transition from feudalism to democracy.

Private property was considered a human right and recognized by democratic states. Business could constitute itself as a *private entity*, often with "limited liability" legal status, while government would take care of the *public goods*, mainly the commons of society and nature. While J.J. Rousseau's concept of the Social Contract took hold, classical economists Adam Smith and Karl Marx recognized the importance of property. Without property rights, there are no incentives for people to invest in risk-bearing enterprises and innovation. Thus, over time, private ownership became the central pillar under free market capitalism.

In this conception, business can extract resources from nature and society, in exchange for paying taxes, generating incomes for employees, producing products and delivering services, and conducting research and development for innovation. In turn, the government uses taxpayers' money to create the enabling conditions for the private sector, such as infrastructure, education, and health care for the companies and employees to flourish. Decisions about production, consumption and resource allocation are left to the private sector, while the public sector takes care of the commons.

This arrangement was considered mutually beneficial – both sides give and take, and the end result is supposed to be a net positive. The competitiveness of free markets will ensure that the fittest will win, which in turn will ensure that there will be optimal outcomes for all parties involved, adding up to an increase in national income, employment and other societal benefits.

While this division of responsibility enabled the private sector to flourish, it caused us to believe that business and society are separate domains. Private business

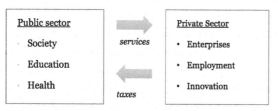

Figure 4.3 The Social Contract

owners were allowed to extract resources from nature and society and utilize them for business goals, as long as the government did not explicitly prohibit this. For a long period, extracting resources from the natural world – seemingly indefinitely – did not seem to be problematic.

Opening the curtains

It is of course a fantasy that business and society can be separated. Business has always been a major driver of socio-economic value and its capacity to create social and economic value has always been a predictor of good business results, especially in the long term.[2] Companies create this value by providing jobs, training workers, building infrastructure, making efficient use of natural resources and expanding access to products and services. In this way, companies impact the lives of people in significant ways: people's assets, skills, opportunities and quality of life can all grow because of what companies do.

Conversely, business cannot succeed without relying on social and environmental "assets" such as infrastructure, tax systems, education, health systems, protection of natural resources such as clean air, water and soil, to name a few. The health and well-being of society is firmly related to the firm's bottom line. To assume otherwise is to hold a warped view of reality.

Yet, surprisingly, it took us until 1987 before we conceived of a term to describe the relationship between business and its enabling environment: *sustainable development*. The World Commission on Environment and Development, chaired by Gro Harlem Brundtland, defined sustainable development as "development that meets the needs of the present without compromising the ability of future generations to meet their own needs".

This is the most cited definition of sustainable development to date – for good reasons, because there were two distinct elements that changed the way we think about economic development. First, there is the need to impose *limits* on economic development, in order to preserve the social and environmental assets that make economic development possible. The environment and human actions do not exist separately from each other. Hence, human development influences our environment continuously and vice versa. Said differently, we are part of an interdependent living system in which we create value (or destroy value, for that matter) together.

Second, there is the serving of *needs*. The understanding here is that we need to take care of the basic needs of people (food, health, shelter etc.), in contrast to luxury needs (or "wants"), which are considered optional. Economic development facilitates the fulfilment of those basic needs. But these needs are not limited to a small number of people living now – we need to preserve resources for the benefit of countless next generations.

This definition granted leaders worldwide with a new perspective on the purpose of economic development. It became the start of new narrative that goes beyond the classical idea of a man trying to control nature and exploit its resources for maximum utility now. All human beings have the opportunity to live in freedom and affluence, in harmony with each other and the environment.

The subordination of the Growth Triangle

It is now commonly understood that sustainable development requires an integrated approach, simultaneously focusing on environmental, societal and economic objectives. All three objectives are considered important and necessary, but the role of economic growth is essentially subordinated to the other goals: it is a means to serve the overarching goal of sustainable development.

The Brundtland Report was the first official international recognition of the fact that the Growth Triangle represents a too narrow perspective on development, failing to meet objectives of sustainable development. It marked the end of universal applicability of the Growth Triangle.

Meanwhile, the new perspective has culminated in the 17 Sustainable Development Goals of the United Nations. We should note that economic development is still very much part of the SDGs themselves, for example, SDG 8 targets the need for sustainable economic growth. But the implication of having accepted all 17 objectives is that economic development is now placed within the larger context of sustainability.

We have evolved from a model that pursued economic growth as its prime objective, measured in efficiency, to a framework that generates sustainable development, measured in both efficiency and resilience for all stakeholders of the system. It generates economic prosperity, societal well-being and environmental health. This is represented by the Circle of Sustainability.

We can sum up this section with the words of philosopher Jeremy Lent:

The old worldview of separation has expired. It's not just dangerous, leading us to the precipice of ecological devastation and climate

Figure 4.4 The Circle of Sustainability

breakdown – it's plain wrong. Modern scientific findings from fields as diverse as systems theory, complexity science, cognitive anthropology, and evolutionary theory all point to the same fundamental insight that wisdom traditions such as Buddhism, Taoism, and Indigenous knowledge have been telling us for millennia: that our very existence arises from our interconnectedness – within ourselves, with each other, and with the living Earth.[3]

Shift 2 (Consciousness): From "Homo economicus" to "Homo sapiens"

The roots of modern economics are often traced back to the 18th-century philosopher Adam Smith, who said in *The Wealth of Nations*:

> It is not from the benevolence of the butcher, the brewer, or the baker that we expect our dinner, but from their regard of their own interest. We address not to their humanity but to their self-love, and never talk to them of our own necessities, but of their advantages.[4]

Subsequent economists have interpreted this as the most fundamental principle of economics: *people are actuated only of self-interest and their own needs* and don't look further than results directly impacting and benefiting themselves.[5] Thus, the economist profession focused on the intersection between humans in markets, while their relationship with the larger environment fell outside the scope of their concern.

We now know that Adam Smith had a larger perspective on markets and society than the above words suggests, as explained in his book *Theory of Moral Sentiment*, written 17 years before *The Wealth of Nations*. What Adam Smith actually meant to say was that self-interest and delivering value for others *go together*: sellers and buyers need each other; they act from mutual interest in the relationship that they share and depend upon. However, the interpretation of *people actuated only of self-interest* became fashionable among economists and found itself as a leading economic paradigm in the metaphor of the *homo economicus*, along with axioms such as the invisible hand of the market, private ownership and material growth. Adam Smith's "ubiquitous" invisible hand is actually mentioned only once in his book.

While the model of the homo economicus started out in economic theory, this became so pervasive in our thinking that it has become a widely accepted account of how to understand human behavior. In general terms, the homo economicus is characterized by the following features:

- Relying on rational decision-making
- Acting as an independent individual agent
- Motivated by maximizing personal gain (or "utility")

In this conception, human beings are solitary individuals who seek maximum *utility*: consumers maximize utility (through consumption) while producers maximize profit. But *ultimately*, all individuals are viewed as utility-maximizers. This logic helped economists to conceive of a natural balance between supply and demand – the search for utility by buyers and sellers is mutually beneficial.

However, in spite of pervasiveness, the model of the *homo economicus* has been refuted by modern science. Neuroscience and behavioral psychology indicate that the model is a mere intellectual construct that does not exist in reality.[6] Human beings are in essence social creatures, continuously subjected to emotional and social influences.[7] And we are not only motivated by personal gain. People are formed by and dependent on their families, communities and society at large. For many people, the need to give and share is stronger than the need to take. When we make decisions to buy, we do this with our peers and families in mind and in our heart. Even Adam Smith, who was the first to suggest that people's selfish concerns could create collective market welfare, affirmed that emotions of sympathy and empathy bind society together.[8]

It's not just that people fall short of the "ideal" of perfect rationality due to various emotional and cognitive "biases". While that is true, more deeply, the *ideal* of rational optimizers as a basic starting point for thinking about humans is flawed – it paints an overly reductionist picture.[9]

While this is a known scientific fact since the 1970s[10], the misconception is more extensive than previously assumed. On a macro level, we see economic policymakers typically operating with the rational agent in mind when they speak of growing GDP, downplaying the risks of climate change or suggesting we close our borders in the face of immigration. We see business leaders think in similar terms, when they speak about downsizing organizations, growing market shares and increasing sales margins. Likewise, homo economicus is projected on workforce and executive compensation issues, when they speak about salary caps and financial bonus schemes.

All this causes organizations to get stuck in a self-fulfilling prophecy. Scholars Robert Quinn and Anjan Thakor describe this dynamic as follows: "Most management practices and incentives are based on conventional economic logic, which assumes that employees are self-interested agents. And that assumption becomes a self-fulfilling prophecy".[11] Jeremy Lent builds on this by indicating the dual feedback loop of cognitions – inside out and outside in – shapes our cultural and historic narratives.[12] We become what we believe we are.

On a deeper level, by focusing on the consumptive nature of human beings, we have allowed human beings to be reduced to the stereotype of the consumer. In reality, consumption is only one part of a functioning of the human being, who also plays the role as citizen, parent, employee, community member, nature lover and retiree. A human being is much more than someone who wants to consume every day, and grow his consumption by drinking ever more liters of soft drinks, using ever higher frequencies of shower gel, always buying the latest mobile devices and wanting to drive the newest cars models. By defining human beings as consumption units and merely focusing on their consumption capacity, we ignore a large part of reality. We overlook our qualities to love, connect, belong, create, take care and make meaning.[13]

Economists John Kay and Mervyn King write: "Humans are not merely defective versions of computers". Rather, we excel at "finding ways to cope with open-ended mysteries ... How to think about and cope with mysteries is the essence of managing life in the real world".[14]

Indeed, in the following chapters we will see that with a more accurate understanding of human nature, we can build a more optimistic picture for humanity to build a sustainable world.

Science: Survival of the fittest and competition

Charles Darwin's theory of evolution with its central premise that humans, just like all species, are driven by *the survival of the fittest* added the notion of 'competition and individualism' as a natural feature of economies.[15] This gave us a scientific narrative for placing humans in the center of the universe – the anthropocentric worldview. It made it natural to regard ourselves as a self-centered species that is driven by satisfying its own needs and interest even if this means we hurt other species.

Even though this was a narrow interpretation of Darwin's theory, ignoring other key Darwinian ideas such as resilience, mutual aid, empathy and cooperation, it fitted conveniently into the emerging paradigm of market economics.[16] Markets were conceived as the natural competitive arena for the "fittest" to achieve maximum gain for each player.

Homo sapiens

So the question arises: what is true human nature? Are *Homo sapiens* capable of putting themselves at the service of sustainable development? What does the new science tell us about human potential?

Well, modern neuroscience acknowledges that we do have instinctive thoughts that tell us that we are alone on the planet, that our individual needs are more important than those of others, and that rational calculations are the best way to determine the best buck for our buy. In other words, we do have traits of the *homo economicus*. But this reflects only part of our brain and biological make up.

> That human beings are motivated solely by their own self-interest is one of the most pernicious ideas to make it into popular consciousness. Modern economics relies on this premise, which has been used to justify the extreme and inhumane trends of modern capitalism. It is, however, false. Modern anthropology and neuroscience show that cooperation is a defining characteristic of humanity. It's time to replace this idea of the self-interested individual with a more complex understanding of who we are – not just because it can lead to a better world, but because it's based on better science.
>
> *(Jeremy Lent, the Patterning Instinct)*[17]

According to neuroscientist Iain McGilchrist, rational thoughts are associated with the left side of our brain.[18] The other, right side of the brain, which evolutionary speaking is older than the right side of our brain, operates on different principles: it is more intuitive, emotional and thinks in larger social contexts and relationships.[19] You could say the left brain is associated with IQ intelligence, while the right side of the brain represents skills that make us relate to the context. The left brain makes us smart, but the right brain makes us wise.

Psychologist Robert Sternberg writes:

> The classical IQ is what helps us to solve problems that follow familiar or easily learned patterns. It doesn't work so well for the complex, highly novel, high-stakes, often emotionally charged problems we frequently face – how to balance the demands of individual liberty and public health in the covid-19 pandemic, for example, or how best to motivate action on global climate change and the other environmental challenges we face.[20]

As Sternberg says, "we got intelligence all wrong: we have developed a conception of intelligence that is narrow, questionably scientific, self-serving and ultimately self-defeating". Instead, he says, we should redefine intelligence essentially as an ability to adapt to the environment, which makes people able to learn, reason, solve problems and make decisions that fit their real-life circumstances.

Science: The *Homo sapiens* and cognition

A recent groundbreaking discovery of neuroscience concerns the brain's potential to grow and develop new qualities. Technically this is known as neuroplasticity, which means that brains not only constantly change, but – most significantly – that they can be *consciously* changed from the inside out.[21] This means that our identity, beliefs and character are not static and fixed – we're constantly changing and evolving through neurological and social-emotional learning processes.[22] This echoes the principles of the self-organization theory.

Moreover, which is perhaps the most important insight in modern science: we have a large degree of freedom to participate in this process. We have the capacity to become aware of our environment and ourselves, and adjust our mindsets accordingly.[23] The Santiago theory of cognition, in particular, identifies cognition (the process of knowing) with the very process of life.[24] We are *Homo sapiens* after all – with "sapiens" translated as "knowing" or "consciousness". Because of our ability to observe ourselves, our capacity to reflect and *be aware*, we don't need to necessarily rely on just a small part of our capacities: by developing our consciousness we can choose to grow our capacity and become more whole and integrated.[25] This is a unique human quality: to be aware and reflect on our beliefs, values, intentions, actions and actively change them for the better. This makes humans truly adaptive.

The historian Yuval Noah Harari, author of the bestselling book *Homo Sapiens*, argues that "for every dollar and every minute we invest in improving artificial intelligence, it would be wise to invest a dollar and a minute advancing human consciousness".[26] This is not an abstract point. As we will discover in Part 3, "advancing human consciousness" is very much a possibility for us – and one with fundamental implications for business leadership and strategy.

Shift 3 (Centeredness): From "Nature is Free" to "Planetary health"

Our economic and business models fail to recognize the dependency of humans on nature and its natural limitations. In classical economics, we have assumed that the fruits of nature are a public good – they have no financial price. What's worse, because we don't pay a price for them, we have come to regard nature as "worthless".

UN Secretary General António Guterres perhaps best sums up the result of this error: "Humanity is waging war on nature. This is senseless and suicidal. The consequences of our recklessness are already apparent in human suffering, towering economic losses and the accelerating erosion of life on Earth".

In this respect, we are destroying our own home, which is an indication that we have lost our center. We are in violation of the principle of centeredness, one of the six principles of life.

In theory, the price of market transactions is supposed to reflect the true costs of product or services. In reality, there are many so-called economic *externalities*, both environmental and social. For example, a firm that produces pesticides for farmers may not be accountable for all the negative side effects of the product on the quality of the soil and the water and the health of the people.

Organization: Bayer Monsanto acquisition

In 2018 the German pharma and chemical concern Bayer acquired the American firm Monsanto for US$ 54 billion. Monsanto produces the pesticide Roundup. This product became the subject of thousands of lawsuits, because it is believed to cause a form of cancer known as non-Hodgkin's lymphoma.[27] Bayer settled the lawsuits for $20 billion, which covers an estimated 95,000 cases of claims from Roundup customers who are affected. This is one-third of the acquisition price, but this is not yet completely closed. As a result, in 2021, Bayer reserved an amount of US$ 23 billion for further legal settlements, which is ten times higher than the amount they had anticipated to reserve a year earlier. This is indeed a true "externality". Does the amount compensate for all the loss in health that Roundup has created (and still creates – because the product is still on the market)? Meanwhile, the Monsanto acquisition is considered the most disastrous acquisition of all time. Nonetheless, Bayer felt it was warranted to issue dividends to its shareholders, because the "underlying business fundamentals are sound". What's going on here?

Economic "externalities" are everywhere. With every act of consumption, some sort of waste is created. For instance, for all the fuel we consume in a given day, we do not account for extra CO2 emission in the atmosphere. The trouble is that these costs are real in the sense that someone has to pay its prize or restore the damage done. The people who carry the burden of these costs are often powerless groups in low-income communities or in developing countries. Think of people living next to a polluting factory or smallholder farmers in Africa, or to those who live on islands affected most by the climate crisis. Sometimes the victims are not discernable as individuals, such as the next generation, who will suffer from a decline in public health, the painful effects of global warming and the loss of the natural environment in general.

Even if we realize that natural resources and biodiversity may be public goods without a price, the trouble is that most of them are not infinite nor are they renewable. Yet, we cannot live without them. Fruits of nature may be without price but they are "priceless". Biologist E.O. Wilson wrote: "We should preserve every scrap of biodiversity as priceless while we learn to use it and come to understand what it means to humanity".[28]

By delineating the roles of the public and private sector, the Social Contract enabled people to be protected against the whims of oppressive regimes. At the same time, as it ignored the context of planetary health, the Social Contract has failed to protect us from the destructive effects on nature from our own activity. We can forgive Jean-Jacques Rousseau for this omission, who conceived of the Social Contract in 1762, at a time before the industrial revolution when nature seemed abundantly available. But 2.5 centuries later, it is high time that we reconceive this arrangement by aligning it with the reality of planetary boundaries. We should redefine it as the *social and natural contract.*

Planetary health

The root of the word "health" is in fact etymologically related to the word "whole" – represented by our planet. If humanity wants to stand a chance to survive on this planet, the new business paradigm should be built on respecting planetary boundaries, which are implicit in the SDGs (which we presented in Chapter 1).

The reality of the planetary boundaries demands business to broaden its circle of concern: it can no longer hide behind a limited version of reality that ignores the long-term negative effects of business on society, planet and ecosystems. We should turn so-called externalities into internalities – making them inclusive to the system that business is a part of. For example, carpet manufacturer Interface transformed waste streams into valuable inventory that they remain responsible for. They created a business model that is completely waste-free. This paved the way for a movement known as "circular economy", which ensures that companies can thrive within the available and finite resources of the planet.

Organization: Interface

Interface is specialized in floor-covering products and especially in carpet tiles, also known as modular carpets, for commercial and residential markets. In 1994, the founder Ray Anderson received a letter from a client asking about what Interface was doing for sustainability. Anderson did not know how to reply. In his biography, he writes:

> In all my working life, thirty-eight years at the time – I had never given a thought to what I or my company were taking from the earth, or doing to it, except to comply with all the many rules and regulations

that government agencies seemed to love to send our way.(…) It was someone else's problem, not mine.[29]

He had a promise to himself: he would integrate principles of sustainability into his business, without compromising his ability to do business.

Look around and you'll see many of the same signs of extinction of natural resources. We're going to keep making carpet tiles. But we're going to shoulder our ecological responsibilities, too. Every business has three big issues to face: what we take, what we make with all that energy and material; and what we waste along the way. (…) I don't mean to quit doing business. I won't give up a single order, not one bit of market share. But I'm convinced that being a good steward of the earth can be good business, too.

It was a bold statement, made at a time when Anderson and his team were used to produce a totally unnatural and unsustainable product – plastic carpets. They had no idea how to achieve their goal. Yet in spite of this, Anderson felt that there should be a way forward.

Yet they found a way. They pioneered by user-oriented product service systems (leasing instead of selling) and recycling on seven fronts: elimination of waste, no harmful emissions, use of renewables, closing the loop, resource-efficient transportation, educating stakeholders and redesign of commerce to create value. They also set zero-targets such as zero waste and zero greenhouse gas (GHG) emissions and built programs such as "Factories to Zero", "Suppliers to Zero" and "Products to Zero".

The rest, they say, is history. Interface grew to become the largest carpet-tile maker on the planet. In 2019, 90% of Interface's energy came from renewables. In 2006 and 2016, Interface was voted number one in Globescan's survey of environmentally sustainable businesses.

Interface has been followed by many other companies. A decade ago, the Danish energy company Ørsted (formerly Dong) committed to a vision of the world that runs entirely on renewable energy. It subsequently sold all its fossil fuel assets and turned to operate offshore and onshore wind farms, solar farms and bioenergy plants so as to provide entirely green energy products to its customers. It's now recognized as the world's most sustainable energy company.[30]

In 2019 Microsoft was the first company to embed internal pricing to reward carbon reductions across all its businesses. The accounting industry followed suit: PwC, in partnership with Microsoft, published a framework of the Building Blocks for Net Zero Transformation.[31] Accountants such as PwC are making attempts to develop a *true price* of a product, which is the market price plus the unpaid so-called external costs.[32] True pricing will help to make all costs – including hidden costs – made in the production of goods and services visible.

One aspect is to define the fruits of nature as "natural capital" and make it at par with social and financial capital. The Natural Capital Coalition that arose out of extensive consultation process of sustainable business stakeholders came to the following definition: "Natural capital is another term for the stock of renewable and non-renewable resources (e.g. plants, animals, air, water, soils, minerals) that combine to yield a flow of benefits to people".[33] Obviously, nature is more than natural capital – it's not reducible to "financial value" in this way – but the concept of natural capital is an important way to recognize the immense value of nature in a business context.

Shift 4 (Connectedness): From "Shareholder first" to the "Stakeholder model"

Early economists conceived of capital as the engine to power the market economy. Adam Smith defined capital, which is derived from a Latin term referring to cattle, as the "stock of assets accumulated for productive purposes". Even though Smith recognized the equal importance of workers as another factor of production, capital was to be the magic ingredient that would boost productivity and create added value.[34]

This magic power of capital has given capitalism its name. Thus, by definition, the owners of capital – which in the business context are the shareholders – have a powerful role as well. The shareholders are those who provide the capital to the business, so that the business can play its magic of increasing both work and capital. Since shareholders provide for the capital, they have been considered supreme among all stakeholders in business. They provide life to the economic cycle, which provides employment and income, and – if business goes well – provides more money for the shareholders.

The value of the shareholder is reflected in the share price of the company. Therefore, shareholders are generally motivated to maintain and possibly enhance the share price or shareholder value. This principle functioned well in times when companies were small, shareholders were family and/or community-based, and the profits for shareholders were relatively modest. There were times in which shareholders actually "shared" in the success of the entire company and its context – hence the term "shareholder". Shareholders could perhaps even be defined as "*care*holders", because many of them tended to actually care for the company. (This exemplifies "connectedness", one of the six principles of life.)

With the advent of globalization, emerging markets, quarterly reporting and new data-driven technology, the shareholder value model is unrecognizable from what it looked like in the old days. In publicly listed companies, shareholders typically are anonymous groups represented by proxy votes of institutional investors (often managed by an algorithm), who don't seem to care for anything much except for the financial yield of their shares. Instead of maintaining value, the game became maximizing shareholder value. This is known as the "shareholder primacy model". In this logic, the competitive nature of markets will ensure that the most efficient company will create the most shareholder value.

Because of quarterly reporting norms, shareholder value creation has become a short-term game. In addition, the globalization of capital has made this a global game: most globalized countries have accepted international accounting practices and foreign investment laws, so that investors can easily invest across borders and compare the efficiency of their investments. In the process, shareholder rights have been enshrined into national and international laws. These conditions favoring shareholder capital have been a driving force behind the growth in free-market economies. As a result, the connectedness to other stakeholders has gradually eroded.

We have observed that top executives, especially in the larger publicly listed companies, find it really difficult *not* to follow short-term shareholder interests. When companies go public, they almost always promise to financial analysts in their offering documents to deliver shareholder returns. In addition, in most companies executive compensation is linked to the share price. Thus, in spite of a trend toward sustainable finance, for most executives the default mode is still to make trade-offs in favor of the short-term shareholder value.

Organization: Cadbury

In 2009 the English chocolate factory Cadbury, founded 186 years ago, was sold to the American firm Kraft Food (Kraft Heinz). This prompted the two most senior Cadbury directors to express their concern in an article for the Daily Telegraph: "Value is a reflection of the reputation and the trust that the company had built up over the generations. Trust, reputation and consumers are intrinsically connected", they wrote. Cadbury was founded by George and Richard Cadbury based on a number of Quaker principles: behave with integrity, do business with honesty and use your wealth for the benefit of the company, its employees and the community.

At the end of the 20th century, at the height of the industrial revolution, Cadbury developed the Bourneville estate in Birmingham, which was a model village designed to provide the company's employees with healthy living conditions. In this region, it was Cadbury that built the first schools, the first pension fund, the first sports facilities, the first bathhouse and offered workers the first free days off from work.

With the acquisition of Cadbury by Kraft Food, these century-old values were abandoned in favor of the modern shareholder model. There was opposition from workers, communities and local government, but the promise of more shareholder value silenced these voices of concern. In 2011, after Mondelez acquired Kraft Food, the company implemented a

US$ 3 billion cost-cutting program and began shifting production to low-labor cost countries. The closure of Cadbury factories generated outcries from the local populations, but the plan received approval from several key market shareholders.[35]

This is an example of a company that had a social purpose when it was founded, but it has gradually yielded to the shareholder first model.

This case study illustrates that this trend was a stark deviation of how historically companies had been operating: for the most part, they were run with a view of serving more than short-term shareholder needs. Many entrepreneurs had a much broader view: creating valuable products, serving stakeholders such as clients, employees and communities.[36] There were many companies that took care of their employees with pension funds, insurance and healthcare programs, as well as investing in the communities with housing and education.

Stakeholder model

The stakeholder theory was developed by the scholar Edward Freeman in 1984, which defines a stakeholder as "any group or individual who can affect or is affected by the achievement of the organizational objectives".[37] According to this theory, which in line with the principle of connectedness, value creation is a process involving a multitude of stakeholders, including shareholders, employees, customers, suppliers, governments and civil society.

There is an entire business movement that is based on the principles of serving the stakeholder rather than the shareholder: B Corp started in 2006 as a certification to identify business leaders who demonstrate that their companies deliver value to all of their stakeholders, not just their shareholders – to maximize value, not just profits. B Corps evolved in to an advocacy movement to counter the growing doctrine of shareholder primacy. They help governments to pass benefit corporation legislation jurisdictions that allows corporations to make themselves legally accountable to create value for their stakeholders. The B Corp movement is now comprised of over 10,000 Certified B Corps and benefit corporations combined across 150 industries and 60 countries.[38] NGOs are also increasingly multi-stakeholder platforms and that cross-sectoral partnerships are required to address SDGs.

French dairy company Danone, which is the first multinational company that obtained a B-Corps certification in 2019, explain their mission as follows:

> In this increasingly complex world, big brands and companies are fundamentally challenged as to whose interests they really serve. ... the best way for our brands and our company is to reinforce trust with employees, consumers, partners, retailers, civil society and governments.[39]

Shift 5 (Competence): From "Markets are (self-regulatory) transactions" to "Markets are (generative) relationships"

Markets are the place where companies compete with each other. The most competent among them will be the most successful business. In turn, markets will stimulate the competence of business.

The idea is that free-market competition will generate the most efficient outcomes for consumers and society. This is considered a self-regulatory process – also known as "the invisible hand", which is a cornerstone of classical economics. This is Adam Smith's ideal of "peoples' self-interests drive our common interest" in action. Markets are the place where transactions between buyers and sellers take place, benefitting both buyers and sellers. The role of governments is merely to provide an enabling environment. In this theory, markets are *transactional exchanges* to trade services and products in exchange for money, or *financial value*.

This theory ignores the fact that the transaction arises out of and/or creates a relationship between the players in the market. To illustrate this, when a company decides to create a product, they need to think about the needs of customers and how the product can satisfy these needs. This is a creative and relational act that takes place before any transaction takes place. Also, after the transaction has been completed, the act of creation by the seller has left an impact on the buyer.

If we focus on the transactional exchange, it is enough to look at the financial value (single) that has been created. However, if we consider that buyers and sellers enter into a relationship, values (plural) come into the picture. Values tend to arise out of a *relationship* between people, and speak, ultimately, to matters of the heart – they go beyond mere financial value.

In contrast to the plural "values", the concept of single "value" has been adopted by business and evolved over time, leading to the common understanding that value is generated as a result of a transaction, regardless of the relationship underlying the transaction. Moreover, by ignoring the relational nature of markets, we have come to see markets as neutral value-free exchanges that function efficiently without moral constraints.[40] We have started to believe that markets will take care of themselves, just like an engine that runs after you have switched it on, regardless of the relational and social (and therefore moral) context in which it operates. In the process, the connection between value and values has been entirely lost.

As a result of considering markets as neutral value-free transactions, we have seen the arrival of laissez-faire economics and neoliberal thinking, trusting the power of unfettered competition. This played into the convenience of policymakers and the general populations: we could leave our worries to the "invisible hand" – even if history is full of market failures, speculation, monopolies and other excesses, indicating that markets don't automatically evolve into an efficient equilibrium, where the interests of all market players are automatically fulfilled. In spite of repeated market failures requiring governments to bail out losers and regulate excessive winners, the paradigm of "free market" remained intact.

This laissez-faire attitude had an interesting and far-reaching by-effect: it has allowed business to invent the field of *marketing*, derived from the words *market getting*, as a discipline to secure growth of consumption in a profitable way. In spite of our belief in self-regulatory markets, we have allowed one group (the marketers and advertisers) to intervene in markets by manipulating consumer interests and needs.

Organization: Coca Cola & the success marketing

The *Coca Cola* brand epitomizes the success of the marketing view. In 2013, Coke products were sold in over 200 countries worldwide, with consumers drinking more than $1.8 billion company beverage servings each day. The brand is widely recognized as a symbol of American values of freedom and happiness.

The cause of this success lies in the company's marketing strategy, which managed to transform the consumer perception of a weird looking brown liquid, originally intended as a medicinal drink (though with an interesting cooling effect), into an iconic brand. It is a testimony of Coca Cola's pervasive marketing and advertisement strategy: For instance, the image of Santa Claus as an old man in a red-and-white suit was invented by Coca Cola. The brand used Santa in their winter campaigns in the 1930s to stimulate consumer uptake during a season in which people traditionally did not want to drink cold beverages. Deviating from one of the premises under standard economic theory, brands such as Coca Cola have demonstrated that consumer preferences are not fixed. Deliberate marketing can change them.

Companies such as Coca Cola have become so good at this that consumption grows every year to incredible heights. For example, in the US soda industry the amount of consumption per capita reached 227 liters, or 620 milliliters per day, in 2000.[41] Today, 17 years later the overall consumption of soft drinks is 359 liters per capita per year, which is an increase in consumption of 58% or 3.4% per year. While the success of marketing is stunning, we can question the sustainability of this approach. How much more can we consume?

Marketing has proven to be so successful that it has contributed to the *consumerization* of the entire society. The pursuit of happiness through consumerism has become a dominant global trend, affecting all people regardless of nationality, culture, religion, age and gender. Madeline Levine observed that the rise of the consumption culture has eroded traditional values – "a shift away from values of community, spirituality and integrity toward competition, materials and disconnection".[42]

Scholar Jason Hickel takes this to the systems level, summing it up as follows: "If your economy requires people to consume things they don't need or even want, and to do more of it each year than the year before, just in order to keep the whole edifice from collapsing, then you need a different economy".[43]

Markets are (generative) relationships

What is the positive way of looking at markets? What are the new beliefs that help us build sustainable markets? The new view is to see markets as the place where people meet, trusted relationships are established, communities are formed, products are tested and innovation takes place.

When people have a sense of relationship and community, they feel responsible and care for each other. This does not happen when people enter into a transaction. In fact, the idea of a relationship can reveal a reality that remains hidden from the transactional approach – a reality relevant to business.

To illustrate this, there are many essential needs in society that remain under-served. There are 800 million who go to bed hungry every night, while there are more than 2 billion people who are overweight or obese. This is a reality that many consumers deplore and feel ashamed about. Many of them are aware of the negative consequences of rampant consumption, while social inequality and ecological destruction are on the rise. The interests of consumers go beyond the consumption culture. There is compelling evidence that consumers increasingly consider the social and environmental effects of their products choices.[44] It's worth thinking: what will the concerns (material, societal) of the typical consumer be in 2030?

Organization: Nestlé and creating shared value

Harvard scholars Michael Porter and Mark Kramer, in an article published in HBR in 2011 that received much attention from business, propose that we move from the concept of CSR to a process of "creating shared value" with society, or CSV.[45] They recommend that we reconsider the purpose of markets as a marriage between profit and purpose. "A narrow conception of capitalism has prevented business from harnessing its full potential to meet society's broader challenges. The opportunities have been there all along but have been overlooked", they write.

Michael Porter's concept of CSV has been derived from Michael Brabeck, CEO of Nestlé who introduced a new strategy in the Nestlé dairy value chain with a long-term view on creating competitive advantage. He decided that rather than squeezing our margins from their supply chain, Nestlé should invest in their suppliers because Nestlé provided refrigeration units, veterinary care and agricultural training to their dairy farmers in India's Moga district. So Nestlé made sure that their suppliers have phones and their homes have electricity and telephones. Their villages have primary schools and many have secondary schools. Moga has five times the number of doctors as neighboring regions.

As Brabeck explained, Nestlé's motivation was not simply philanthropy, but an *investment in the relationships* with people who make up their value chain. Nestlé realized that without healthy and strong suppliers, Nestlé's supply chain would not be strong and competitive enough in the face of increasing global competition. At the same time, it trusted that consumers would reward Nestlé for its fair treatment of suppliers. For that purpose, the brand Nespresso was repositioned in the market as a luxury product. It did so with the help of a global PR campaign featuring Hollywood movie star George Clooney. This enabled the company to increase the margins of its products that Nestlé sold to the consumer – thus *expanding the amount of value generated.*

By allowing their suppliers and customers to partake in the value creation process, this case is an example of the *relational and generative power of markets.* By strengthening its relationships with consumers and suppliers, Nestlé's demonstrated market leadership and created shared value for all stakeholders involved.

In the initial phase, CSR was typically focused on transforming the supply chain by reducing the ecological footprint. The case of Nestlé signifies the next stage in business sustainability by taking the *value-chain approach,* which consists of the entire stakeholder network through which value is created.

The example shows that companies are free to step out of the purely transactional market approach and organize their supply and demand in the way that fits them best. The value chain approach – based on recognizing the underlying human relationships – will reveal a perspective that can empower companies to tackle larger social and environmental issues affecting the entire value chain and turn them into market opportunities that benefit both business and society. This will determine the next level competence that business will need to develop.

Shift 6 (Creativity): From "Short-term output" to "Long-term impact"

The principle of creativity shows up in the way we look at what results the company is creating. The results of business are traditionally expressed in terms such as profits, turnover, EBITDA,[46] ROI,[47] discounted cash flows or price earning ratios. These are so-called output goals, measured on a yearly (and often quarterly) basis. In this classical conception, business is conceived as a means to transform "inputs" (raw materials, labor, money, information etc.) into "outputs" (products, profits, know-how etc.) through a set of defined strategic activities (production, sales, marketing, innovation etc.).

As long as the company grows its yearly output, in a capital-efficient manner, the business is considered successful. In reality, this is seldom the case. The main reason why we focus on output indicators as a way to measure success is because output is easily quantifiable in monetary terms. Output = money = success.

The problem is that "output" comprises only of the direct and immediate effects of the company activities. The indirect and long-term effects of business activities don't show up in this indicator. In truth, there is no direct relationship between short-term output and long-term value creation. Research shows that more than 50% of a company's value is created by activities that take place three years from now.[48]

Nonetheless, most management incentives provide an opposite effect. CEO's executive compensation is comprised of 50% of stock options in the company, which is a figure that can be easily manipulated by stock-buyback schemes that are unrelated to core business value creation.[49] The average holding period for stocks in professionally managed funds has decreased from seven years in the 1960s to less than one year today.[50] With such limited focus, it is natural that many investors neglect the broader picture of the social-economic context that drives business success.

The short-term pressure has become such that many business leaders don't take the space and time to develop long-term models that address long-term challenges and opportunities. In public companies, 78% of executives would take actions to improve quarterly earnings at the expense of long-term value creation.[51] The current average tenure of CEOs is now only 4.5 years.[52]

Greed is (not) good

What's perhaps most illustrative of the preoccupation with the short-term is that CEO's pay ratio relative to that of employees' has been escalating in dramatic ways. In the United States, the ratio of CEO's pay to typical worker pay rose from 20- or 30-to-1 in the 1960s and 1970s to 200- or 300-to-1 in recent years, which is a tenfold rise in four decades. The average Fortune 500 CEO now makes about $20 million per year, while in a good year this can easily grow to $30 or 40 million.[53] What's going on here? This exponential growth cannot be explained merely by improvements in business performance.[54]

To illustrate this: in ten seconds, Jeff Bezos of Amazon earns more money than the average employee at Amazon makes in an entire year.[55] In 2018, Disney CEO Bob Iger received $65.6 million (1,424 times the average Disney employee). Shareholder Abigail Disney complained that this pay level was "insane". But Bob Iger responded by saying "this is merely exceptional". His normal annual pay is only $39 million.[56]

This rising inequality is a source of major discontent. Paul Krugman, a Nobel Prize-winning economist, said: "Today the idea that huge paychecks are part of a beneficial system in which executives are given an incentive to perform well has become something of a sick joke".[57]

This attitude was well summed up by actor Michael Douglas in the movie Wall Street: "Greed is good".

In 2018, CEOs saw a 17% raise, according to a new analysis from the US Economic Policy Institute. Meanwhile, pay for the remainder of workers grew by a fraction of 1%. The typical CEO made 312 times the earnings of the typical worker.

System: Distortive measures

This flawed logic of focusing on the short-term can also be observed in the way we measure our national accounts.[58] Take the most basic measure of a nation's economic performance, called gross domestic product (GDP). GDP, which is modeled on the profit/loss statement of a company, is calculated by adding up quantifiable economic transactions recorded in the country in a year. Thus, GDP is the indicator of national economic output. This indicator is helpful for governments to know how efficient their investments in public services are, just as shareholders want to know the return on their investments, indicated by profits.

However, there are obvious drawbacks to comparing companies and nations with machines and managing them accordingly. Indicators such as GDP and profit show you how fast the engine is running, but it says nothing about the utility and quality of the output or about conditions and by-effects of running the machine. Thus, GDP (just like profits) is not an adequate measure of value. GDP is incomplete since it excludes, for instance, the "value" of unpaid care work (such as looking after a family member) as well as the value of critical resources such as water, soil and clean air that function as preconditions for operating the machine.

What's worse, GDP is *distortive*: if a government decides overnight to cut down huge swathes of rainforest and sell the timber, this will show up as a large *boost* to that period's GDP even though the actual cost – huge loss of biomass and biodiversity, as well as long-term social and economic losses – may far outweigh the short-term monetary gains. GDP alone cannot measure the citizens' well-being, and the way it is constructed contributes to income disparity, as well as environmental destruction.

Long-term impact

In spite of the sustainability efforts in finance such as ESG reporting and impact investing, it is obvious that this excessive focus on short-term output hinders companies to create long-term sustainable value. Sustainability requires that actions taken today don't compromise the needs of future generations, as was laid down in the Brundtland definition. It's one of the reasons why Paul Polman, early in his tenure as CEO of Unilever, abandoned quarterly profit reporting. This outraged many financial analysts but Polman persisted by stating his motivation that he felt was common sense. "After all, you don't run a business on 90-day cycles. So why should I report on this basis?"[59] The CEO went a step further, urging shareholders to put their money somewhere else if they don't "buy into this long-term value-creation model, which is equitable, which is shared, which is sustainable". "I figured I couldn't be fired on my first day", Polman admitted later.[60]

This example shows that we will need to develop integrated sustainable performance metrics that can effectively counter the perverse short-term incentives of the current system. Short-term output indicators need to be complemented with long-term impact indicators.

Beyond this, we will need to replace the idea that the *objective* of business is to strive for short-term financial results by a more future-fit objective that serves the long-term well-being of the business, its people and the planet. This is what really ensures long term and sustainable success.

Many of us simply don't see the long-term consequences of our actions, so we have a strong preference to deal with the problem and solution right in front of us. The Growth Triangle and consumerism have played into this bias, promising instant monetary rewards and gratification, on the basis of short-term actions and results.

Yet there are plenty of companies that made fortunes by taking a leap into time. Elon Musk started electric car manufacturer Tesla at a time when competing car builders such as Chrysler and Ford were stepping up investments in petrol-intensive SUVs. While Tesla soared to a record market cap of US$ 654 billion, its competitors had to be bailed out by the government. IKEA was ahead of its time when it realized that furniture could become a self-assembled commodity. All the sustainability pioneers mentioned in this book captured a glimpse of the future. They can only do so by resisting immediate gratification and open up to a long-term perspective.

It is helpful to realize that the culture of instant gratification is only a recent phenomenon. There have been many cultures that demonstrated long-term thinking and action. The ancient Iroquois people of North America are a case in point: they propagated a philosophy that the decisions we make today should result in a sustainable world seven generations into the future. This Seventh Generation Principle is not limited to decisions being made about our energy, water and natural resources, but it can also be applied to relationships – every decision should result in sustainable relationships seven generations in the future.[61]

The cathedral of Chartres in France was built over two generations. Chinese policymakers plan for decades ahead. That's why they have become the leading manufacturer of solar panels. This shows that human beings have the capacity for long-term thinking, and indeed, this is demonstrated by leading sustainability companies. They are taking a long-term evolutionary perspective of business, planning for longevity through stakeholder value creation, while serving the ecosystem they are part of.

Organization: Toyota

Toyota, the second largest car manufacturing company in the world, has long been known for its practice of long-term thinking and continuous improvement.[62] It was the first car company to commit to the mass-market adoption of hybrid vehicles across the globe. It formulated a number of environmental challenges that it wishes to overcome by 2050, with as end goal of a "future society in harmony with nature".[63] To that end, in 2018 Toyota rebranded itself as a "mobility" company with a focus on developing new technology to change the way people move.[64] The company website reads:

> To preserve and enhance our co-existence with nature, we need to conserve our forests and other rich ecosystems. We do this through a number of projects at all levels in our organization. In this way we aim to play an active part in improving environmental education and raising awareness to help build a society where people live in harmony with the natural world.[65]

This could have been taken straight from the website of an environmental NGO. Yet the car company is committed to deliver on this vision by continuing to invent carbon-zero cars and other planet-friendly means of mobility, and – unlike an NGO – sell these for a profit. In 2020 the Toyota's hybrid car was the world's top-selling hybrid car, with over ten million units sold worldwide.[66]

Toyota attributes this successful strategy to the principle of Kaizen, a Japanese term meaning "change for the better" or "continuous improvement". The Kaizen philosophy also can be used to improve sustainability practices, as demonstrated by Toyota and many other organizations.[67]

In 2019 French food company Danone decided to create the carbon-adjusted earnings per share (EPS) metric. It's the first time ever for a listed company. They valued the cost of carbon at €35 a ton and deducted that from EPS. Their CEO, Emmanuel Faber, told their shareholders,

> if we pay a dividend to you above that carbon-adjusted EPS, it means that the money that you've put to work with us hasn't finished its work.

We need to make sure that we can continue to pay you dividends in three, four, five, 10 years from now.[68]

This is a very different perspective from traditional shareholder value valuations.

Front running companies such as Danone and Toyota are examples of business leadership demonstrating the courage to move beyond merely chasing short-term output such as quarterly earnings and forecasts for the benefit of shareholders.

The short-term efficiency models can still be of use, but their function has changed from being goals in themselves to being a means to an end: they are indicators of efficiency in support of long-term sustainable development goals. These goals can be defined in terms of Science-Based Targets, an initiative that, amongst others, show companies how much and how quickly they need to reduce their GHG emissions to prevent the worst effects of climate change.[69]

Notes

1 Rousseau, J-J. (1762). *The Social Contract* (French: *Du contrat social ou Principes du droit politique*). Amsterdam: Marc Michel.
2 See, for example: Collins, J., & Porras, J. (1996). *Built to Last – Building Your Company's Vision.* Harvard Business Review; Collins, J. (2002), *Good to Great: Why Some Companies Make the Leap... and Others Don't.* New York: William Collins.
3 www.kosmosjournal.org/kj_article/awakening-to-life/.
4 Smith, A. (2008). *The Wealth of Nations.* New York: Oxford University Press. (Original work published 1776)
5 See for example: Edgeworth, F. Y. (1967). *Mathematical Psychics: An Essay on the Application of Mathematics to the Moral Science.* New York: Augustus M. Kelley Publishers. (Original work published 1881)
6 Gintis, H. (2000). Beyond homo economicus: Evidence from experimental economics. *Ecological Economics, 35,* 311–322; Gintis, H. (2009). *The Bounds of Reason: Game Theory and the Unification of the Behavioral Sciences.* Princeton, NJ: Princeton University Press.
7 Zak, P. J. (2008). *Moral Markets: The Critical Role of Values in the Economy.* Princeton, NJ: Princeton University Press.
8 Adam Smith described this in his book "Theory of Moral Sentiments" which preceded his better known "The Wealth of Nations" that laid out the first principles of modern economics. Smith, A. (2008). *The Wealth of Nations.* New York: Oxford University Press. (Original work published 1776)
9 Kay, J., & King, M. (2020). *Radical Uncertainty: Decision-Making for an Unknowable Future.* New York: W.W. Norton Publishers.
10 Tversky & Kahneman's work in the 1970s.
11 Quinn, R. E., & Thakor, A. V. (2018). Creating a purpose-driven organization. *Harvard Business Review* (July/August issue).
12 Lent, J. (2017). *The Patterning Instinct. A Cultural History of Humanity's Search for Meaning.* New York: Prometheus Books.

13 Tim Kasser's work, in particular, highlights how adopting a *consumerist mindset* serves us poorly when it comes to our well-being. The High Price of Materialism | The MIT Press.

14 Kay, J., & King, M. (2020). *Radical Uncertainty – Decision Making Beyond the Numbers*. New York: W.W. Norton.

15 Darwin, C. (1959). *On the Origin of Species by Means of Natural Selection; Spencer,* Herbert Spencer (1864) *The Principles of Biology.*

16 For more on this see: Loye, D. (2004). Darwin, Maslow, and the fully human theory of evolution. *The great adventure: Toward a fully human theory of evolution,* 20–38.

17 Lent, J. (2017). *The Patterning Instinct. A Cultural History of Humanity's Search for Meaning.* Lanham, MD: Prometheus Books.

18 McGilchrist, I. (2009). *The Master and His Emissary: The Divided Brain and the Making of the Western World.* New Haven: Yale University Press.

19 Davidson, R. J., & Begley, S. (2012). *The Emotional Life of Your Brain: How Its Unique Patterns Affect the Way You Think, Feel, and Live, and How You Can Change Them.* New York: Hudson Street Press; Varela, F., Thompson, E., & Rosch, E. (1991). *The Embodied Mind: Cognitive Science and Human Experience.* Cambridge, MA: MIT Press.

20 Sternberg, R. (2021). We've got intelligence all wrong – and that's endangering our future. *The New Scientist.*

21 Ibid.

22 Maturana, H. R., & Varela, F. J. (1980). *Autopoiesis and Cognition. The Realization of the Living.* Dordrecht: Reidel, p. 13.

23 Davidson, R., & Goleman, D. (2017). *Altered Traits: Science Reveals How Meditation Changes Your Mind, Brain, and Body.* New York, NY: Penguin Books.

24 Maturana, H., & Varela, F. (1987). *The Tree of Knowledge: The Biological Roots of Human Understanding.* Boston: Shambhala Publications.

25 Siegel, D. (2016). *Mind: A Journey to the Heart of Being Human.* New York: W.W. Norton Series on Interpersonal Neurobiology.

26 Harari, Y. N. (2018). *21 lessons for the 21st Century.* London: Jonathan Cape.

27 Chappell, B. (June 24, 2020). "Bayer to Pay more than $10 Billion to Resolve Cancer Lawsuits over Weedkiller Roundup". NPR. Retrieved July 12, 2020.

28 Edward, O. W. (1992). *The Diversity of Life.* Cambridge, MA: Harvard University Press

29 Harel, T., Van Arkel, G., Van Der Pluijm, F., & Aanraad, B. *Interface, The Journey of a Lifetime,* The Natural Step (2013).

30 It is recognized as the world's most sustainable energy company in Corporate Knights' 2021 index of the Global 100 most sustainable corporations.

31 www.pwc.co.uk/services/sustainability-climate-change/insights/accelerating-the-journey-to-net-zero.html.

32 https://truecostsinitiative.org.

33 https://naturalcapitalcoalition.org.

34 Quoted in De Soto, H. (2000). *The Mystery of Capital,* p. 41.

35 Stock, R. (February 19, 2017). www.stuff.co.nz/business/89569042/mondelezs-global-costcutting-drive-behind-dunedin-cadbury-factory-closure

36 Berle, A .A. Jr., & Means, G. C. (1932). *The Modern Corporation and Private Property.* New Brunswick: Transaction Publishers.

37 Freeman, R. E. (1984). *Strategic Management, a Stakeholder Approach.* Boston: Cambridge University Press.

38 https://bcorporation.net.

39 www.danone.com/about-danone/sustainable-value-creation/BCorpAmbition.html.

40 Michael, S. (2013). *What Money Can't Buy: The Moral Limits of Markets*. London: Penguin Books.

41 www.visualcapitalist.com/death-of-soda/.

42 Levine, M. (2007). Challenging the culture of affluence. *Independent School*, 67(1), 28–36.

43 Hickel, J. (2019). Degrowth: A theory of radical abundance. *Real-world Economics Review*, 87, 19 March, 54–68.

44 Joshi, Y., & Rahman, Z. (2015). Factors affecting green purchase behaviour and future research directions. *International Strategic Management Review*, 3(1–2), June–December 2015, 128–143.

45 Porter & Kramer (2011) *The Big Idea: Creating Shared Value*. Harvard Business Review.

46 EBITDA stands for Earnings Before Interest Tax Depreciations and Amortization, a standard accounting term describing company profits.

47 ROI stands for Return on Investment.

48 Koller, T., Manyika, J., & Ramaswamy, S. August 4, 2017. Milken Institute Review. www.mckinsey.com/mgi/overview/in-the-news/the-case-against-corporate-short-termism.

49 https://hbr.org/1990/05/ceo-incentives-its-not-how-much-you-pay-but-how. And also: www.thebalance.com/the-benefits-of-stock-buy-back-programs-356332.

50 Rappaport, A. (2006). *Ten Ways to Create Shareholder Value*, September Harvard Business Review: OnPoint 1, 2–3.

51 Pocock, L. (2013). *Curbing Excessive Short-Termism. A Guide for Boards of Public Companies*, Thought Leadership Paper, Australian Institute of Company Directors.

52 https://corpgov.law.harvard.edu/2018/02/12/ceo-tenure-rates/.

53 www.epi.org/publication/reining-in-ceo-compensation-and-curbing-the-rise-of-inequality/.

54 Bebchuk, L., & Fried, J. (2006). *Pay without Performance: The Unfulfilled Promise of Executive Compensation*. London: Harvard University Press.

55 Business Insider: February 6, 2020 (retrieved from www.businessinsider.nl/how-rich-is-jeff-bezos-mind-blowing-facts-net-worth-2019).

56 Forbes, October 31, 2018.

57 Krugman, P. (2007). *The Conscience of a Liberal*, p.148. New York: W.W. Norton.

58 International Commission on the Measurement of Economic Performance and Social Progress, appointed by President Sarkozy of France (2010), *Mismeasuring our Lives: Why GDP Doesn't Add up*.

59 Polman, P., quoted in Smit J. (2019). *Het Grote Gevecht. Het eenzame gelijk van Paul Polman*. Prometheus (to be printed in English as The Great Fight, forthcoming 2020).

60 www.forbes.com/sites/andyboynton/2015/07/20/unilevers-paul-polman-ceos-cant-be-slaves-to-shareholders/?sh=740b213f561e.

61 This principle has inspired companies to sell "green products" across the world. There is a Seven Generation Company in Vermont formulating plant-based products that are safe and that work, which is appropriately registered as B Corporation.

62 Toyota internal document, "The Toyota Way 2001," April 2001; Liker, J. (2004). *The Toyota Way: 14 Management Principles from the World's Greatest Manufacturer*.

63 www.toyota-europe.com/world-of-toyota/feel/environment/environmental-challenge-2050

64 www.bloomberg.com/news/articles/2020-01-24/why-is-toyota-building-a-smart-city-from-scratch.

65 www.toyota-europe.com/world-of-toyota/feel/environment/environmental-challenge-2050.

66 newsroom.toyota.eu/global-sales-of-toyota-hybrids-reach-10-million/.

67 This is demonstrated by Beaumont Health System, a large health-care provider serving the Detroit suburbs www.greenbiz.com/article/5-lessons-japanese-kaizen-approach-sustainability.

68 *Financial Times* May 8, 2021. Interview with Emmanuel Faber, former CEO Danone.

69 The targets are an initiative of the SBTi which is a partnership between CDP, the United Nations Global Compact, World Resources Institute (WRI) and the World Wide Fund for Nature (WWF). www.sciencebasedtargets.org.

Chapter 5

The new business perspective on value creation

In the chapter we will summarize how the six principles and the six new beliefs (at the macro-level) can be recognized in the manner in which leading companies are transforming toward sustainability (the micro level). Specifically, we will describe how the new paradigm manifests in practices that drive Triple Value creation in companies.

We will explore six business practices that contain the seed for new organizational capabilities that companies will need to develop in the progress toward TVC. These capabilities can also be defined as the new value drivers of TVC companies: instead of driving merely singular financial value for the company, they drive sustainable value for multiple stakeholders in the value chain.

(Here we will specifically address the Organizational level. In Part 3, this discussion will continue on the Self/Leadership-level)

Main business practices of Triple Value creation

The new macro view on value creation has fundamental implications for business. No longer can business leaders speak of value creation without considering the needs of the wider social and environmental system in which they operate. By recognizing the interdependence between business, people and society/ecosystem, business leaders will dramatically expand their awareness and find ways to upgrade their value creation capacity.

According to Michael Porter and Mark Kramer, over the last 20–30 years they have come to think that generating business value is good for society. This is

DOI: 10.4324/9781003119302-8

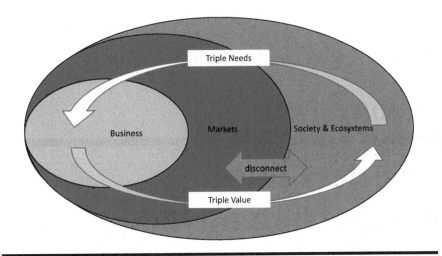

Figure 5.1 Triple Needs and Triple Value

increasingly difficult to maintain because of contradictory evidence (health, financial crisis, pollution, social exclusion etc). We now need to shift this line of thought into: what is good for society is good for business. This opens up a new perspective: there is tremendous opportunity to create economic value by focusing on societal value[1]

The view paves the way for the concept of Triple Value creation (TVC). This concept can best be explained by distinguishing three main stakeholder groups: (1) business shareholders, (2) primary stakeholders such as employees, customers and suppliers (the market), and (3) the wider group of secondary stakeholders representing community, society and the planet. Triple Value will be created by serving the needs of all these groups. This is depicted in the model of Figure 5.1.

Currently, most companies' focus is on creating shareholder value, while CSR tends to focus on serving the needs of secondary stakeholders – community, nature and society. What's often missing from the CSR perspective is value creation for suppliers and customers, as well as employee well-being. Only if we expand value creation to serve all three main stakeholder groups in an integrated manner can sustainability become a part of core business.

TVC rests on the understanding that respecting societal well-being and planetary health is a business survival issue. A healthy business depends on a healthy society, which in turn depends on the health of the environment. TVC is oriented to contributing to the continuity of human civilizations, and therefore the continuity of the firm. Therefore, TVC companies will strive to put the interests of nature and society above all else.

When companies evolve toward TVC, at no stage is a company lifted from the responsibility to refrain from negative impacts from its primary business activities – for example, it will need to continue complying with CSR standards, ethical codes and minimizing ecological footprint. The *do no harm principle* remains on the basis of both CSR and TVC. Only when this is in place can the sustainability strategy grow to the next level of TVC without being rightfully accused of greenwashing.

Now, let's see how can we put this into practice. We will describe the main practices that we have found in companies that move toward TVC, while linking them to the six new beliefs at macro-level. This is expressed in the following table:

	Six principles	The six new beliefs	Business practices
1	Context	Business and Society are One	The value system
2	Cognition	Homo Sapiens	Leadership and Learning Culture
3	Centeredness	Planetary Health	Mission and Values
5	Connection	Multi-stakeholder model	Stakeholder Engagement and Partnerships
5	Competence	Markets are (Generative) Relationships	Innovation: Creating new products and markets
6	Creativity	Long-term (Net-Positive) Impact	Vision and Goals; Performance and accountability

We will review these business practices in some detail. While the business practices generally correspond to the six principles of life and the six new system beliefs, they are all highly related and may have various touch points to all the principles and beliefs.

Context: The value system

Companies that recognize the concept of the value system realize that their value creation process is *the very means for the transformation toward sustainability.*

We have seen that the first new belief – Business and Society are One – expands the context in which the company operates and reveals the various strategic "interdependencies" between the company and its stakeholders.

The key concept here is the "value chain", which allows the business to see how it is strategically linked to consumers, society and the planet, into one integrated framework. Given its systemic nature, we'd better call it the *value system*. It can also be referred to as the value network.

In terms of practice, it is important to note that the view goes beyond the *doing good* principle, which is an "inside-out" approach that was common for CSR. The new perspective implies an *outside-in approach* from the viewpoint that the company is deeply connected to and dependent upon the whole.

When business leadership masters this holistic perspective, they can identify which societal and ecological issues are strategically relevant to the organization.

First, they look at what societal challenges pose a *significant risk* for business. Next, they can start turning societal problems around into market opportunities. This is what we define as the "reframing" of societal issues.

Companies taking this holistic approach understand that there is nothing morally wrong or unethical by linking social benefit to the process of business performance itself. These companies just know that clients and their needs should be at the heart of any value creation model and that sustainability cannot be achieved otherwise. If done well, this should not be diminished as "greenwashing"' – it simply reflects a next stage in the journey toward sustainability, one where more alignment and focus is required. Indeed, we can conclude that taking the value systems view is in the "enlightened self-interest" of business because by serving society in the long run business will benefit as well.

Organization: Lifebuoy soap in India

The Lifebuoy soap brand (owned by Unilever) illustrates how societal issues can be turned into business opportunities by recognizing the value system it operates in.

The Lifebuoy brand aims to make a difference in people's day-to-day lives by selling soap and encouraging handwashing. In developed countries, modern innovations such as sewerage and piped water supplies, together with the widespread adoption of soap, have helped to reduce the incidence of infectious disease and reduce mortality rates from infection to 5% of all deaths. However, in Africa, 65% of deaths are due to infections, while the figure is 35% in Asia, including India.

Among all changes that are needed, handwashing is shown to be the most cost-effective means of preventing infection and saving lives. By washing their hands with soap five times a day, children can be saved from diarrheal deaths.

About a decade ago, Lifebuoy decided to specifically target India, where Lifebuoy created partnerships with the Indian government, NGOs such as Oxfam, UNICEF, the Red Cross, local communities and women's groups. Collectively they created Project Shakti, which employed women in local areas to educate communities and families on the benefits of handwashing, and which also allowed Lifebuoy and its partners access to rural areas. Not only did these thousands of women become a new distribution channel for Lifebuoy, but they were also empowered through earning an income.

While Lifebuoy's sales in India were boosted, there was a marked reduction in the rate of children's deaths. Children had 25% fewer episodes of diarrhea, 15% fewer incidents of acute respiratory infections and 46% fewer eye infections. Children also had a significant reduction in the number of days of school absence due to illness.

Since 2010, 337 million people have been reached through Lifebuoy's handwashing with soap programs, and Unilever's marketing expertise targeting school children and mothers. Lifebuoy brand is now the world's number one antibacterial soap sold in nearly 60 countries.

This is a successful example of how a societal purpose can benefit both business and society.

Consciousness: Leadership and Learning Culture

Companies that are considered leading in sustainability are often *leading on many fronts*. Many have also become leaders in product innovation, brand loyalty, employee engagement and recruiting of talent.

Why is this so? These companies know that sustainability is a journey of transformation, which requires the cultivation of the concomitant qualities of their leadership and staff.

In terms of business practices, they are building a *learning culture for sustainability*. This is best described in the words of Peter Senge, who invented the concept of learning organizations:

> organizations where people continually expand their capacity to create the results they truly desire, where new and expansive patterns of thinking are nurtured, where collective aspiration is set free, and where people are continually learning to see the whole together.[2]

This culture of learning needs to be developed. At the early stage (which we have defined as the "'compliance stage"), the culture tends to be *unconsciously reactive* to issues of sustainability. The company is largely unaware of what sustainability means in the context of its business and will grapple with issues only tactically, in response to an event or immanent need. The first step is for the organization to become aware of its passive and reactive stance, to become *conscious of its reactivity*. At the next stage of the journey (which we have called the stage of CSR), the company starts looking for ways to embed sustainability practices in everyday operations. This phase requires the resilience to overcome difficulties and stay true to its path. The company becomes *consciously proactive*. It slowly begins to deal with sustainability as a way of creating business challenges rather than overcoming challenges to business.

When an organization transitions from unconscious to conscious and from reactive to proactive on sustainability, there are growing pains and pushbacks. The company will discover many things that need to be changed. This requires a strong willingness to learn; it is a time to be courageous and daring, while allowing for failure, knowing that early missteps clarify the way forward.

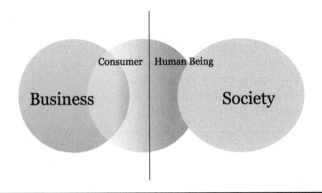

Figure 5.2 Who are we serving?

In the next phase stage of TVC, sustainability and purpose will truly merge; there is no reactivity any longer, enabling the company to take a strategic perspective on sustainability. The culture of learning is now consistent with its professed values and manifests in its behaviors. This allows them to fully anticipate and cocreate the future.

In terms of culture, this implies *openness* to considering a wide spectrum of inputs as the organization becomes proactive on all strategic issues. An organization that is open is one that can candidly assess its current situation and be open to adaptations it may have to embrace in the future. An open organization is receptive to ideas within its walls and beyond. It is unafraid and not threatened by change. It is this very quality that makes these companies leading on many fronts, making them the "brand of choice" and "preferred employers" in the future.

On a deeper level, building such a culture of learning implies that companies abandoned the rather restrictive belief of the "Homo economicus" in favor of the more holistic concept of the "Homo sapiens" (new belief 2). Instead of seeing their staff and clients merely as material assets, TVC companies see them as living human beings, who have an unlimited reservoir of potential for positive action and continuous learning.

The new perspective on human potential opens up many opportunities for business leadership. Not just internal, but also external. For example, we should realize that people are not merely consumers. People are human beings, who also happen to be parents, citizens, taxpayers, employees and shareholders. If we treat people as consumers, we ignore a large part of human needs, talents and potentials.

Therefore, we need to shift from narrow focus on people as *consumers* to seeing people as human beings. Yes, people need food, shelter, water and safety, but they also need health, relationships, community, creative expression and meaning.

The same applies to how we treat employees: it is now widely appreciated that they are not merely driven by financial incentives alone, but also by a desire for belonging, meaning and purpose, which happen to be more powerful motivators for performance than money alone.

The most exciting thought is that we are capable of shaping new futures, new realities and finding solutions to the current challenges that we – as a matter of fact – have created ourselves.

With this enhanced perspective on human potential, business leadership can change the way it views societal problems. Typically, from the homo economicus viewpoint, these challenges were regarded as a threat, invoking a reactive response, leaving it to governments to resolve. From the living systems viewpoint, these challenges can be viewed as an invitation for activating untapped human potential.

Organization: Carlsberg

Carlsberg, the global beer company from Denmark, dedicates a large amount of its profits to science. In 1876, founder Jacob Christiaan Jacobsen transferred the ownership to the Danish Royal Academy of Science, which set up a special foundation to hold the shares of the company. Today 75% of the ownership still is in the hands of this foundation. The CEO of Carlsberg, Cees 't Hart, explains that this structure is one of the most important reasons why people want to work for Carlsberg. "It motivates our people, it is simple as that. Why would you want to work for an investor who wants to buy his third Ferrari with the profits that you help generate?"[3]

When Cees 't Hart started as CEO in 2015, he made sure that Carlsberg defined a purpose that is relevant and understandable to all employees: "We brew for a better today AND tomorrow". Carlsberg Foundation donated 60 million euros to research around COVID-19. "Our people appreciate that a large share of the dividends flows back to society. This makes them feel that they work for a higher purpose than the share price and merely making people richer", said Cees 't Hart.

Centeredness: Mission and values

TVC companies have a strong sense of mission. This is often laid down in a compelling narrative explaining why the company exists. The official mission of Patagonia is: "We're in business to save our home planet".[4] Patagonia's founder Yvon Chouinard explains this as follows: "At Patagonia, we appreciate that all life on earth is under threat of extinction. We aim to use the resources that we have – our business, our investments, our voice and our imaginations – to do something about it".

They excel at cocreating such mission with their employees and customers. When Marc Benioff founded Salesforce 21 years ago, he had a vision of profitability and philanthropy as core pillars of the company's DNA, two ideas he believed didn't have to be mutually exclusive. That took shape as the 1-1-model, which dedicated 1% of the company's equity, 1% of its product and 1% of employees' time back to the community.[5]

In TVC companies, the commitment to societal purpose is made explicit by their leaders. Paul Polman, when he started his role as CEO in Unilever: "As a leader I am *not* guided by the question: what can I do for Unilever? My question is: what can Unilever do for society? And then I ask: how can I support Unilever to fulfill that mission?"[6] Indeed, Polman's mindset became the foundation for Unilever successful transformation into the world's most respected sustainable business, which we highlighted in Part 1.[7]

By linking the needs of society and the world to the purpose of their staff, TVC companies have activated the promise of a *shared purpose* between their employees, the business and society. Recognizing the common humanity between the people who make up the company and society, TVC companies will open many avenues for shared innovation and shared value creation.

Organization: Patagonia

Patagonia was founded by Yvon Chouinard in 1973, who founded the company out of passion for creating tools for rock climbing. Patagonia has grown to become one of the most respected and sought-after outdoor apparel brands in the world. Still an independent, private company, Patagonia's estimated 2017 revenue is $209.09 million and it employs some 1,000 employees.

Patagonia has built its entire business model entirely on the principles of protecting nature. Patagonia considers it a prime stakeholder, not merely its customers but "mother earth". Yvon Chouinard says: "At Patagonia, we appreciate that all life on earth is under threat of extinction. We aim to use the resources that we have – our business, our investments, our voice and our imaginations – to do something about it". Its official mission statement is: "We're in business to save our home planet".[8]

The company lived up to its mission by donating part of revenue to nature, using a high level of environmentally preferred fibers and fighting overconsumption with their "Don't buy this jacket" campaign. They were the first apparel brands vowed to be climate neutral (in their entire value chain) by 2025.

This company has turned the classical economic belief that "nature is free" completely upside down. Patagonia has become an exemplary role model for businesses that want to support planetary health. As an "activist brand", they are challenging other companies to join them in an ecologically conscious business strategy. As such, Patagonia embodies the concept of "Planetary Boundaries".

Business scholars Rajendra Sisodia, David Wolfe and Jagdish Sheth, who researched what made companies attract customers and workers, wrote the following words:

> Today's greatest companies are fuelled by passion and purpose, not cash. They earn large profits by helping all their stakeholders thrive: customers, investors, employees, partners, communities, and society. These rare, authentic firms of endearment act in powerfully positive ways that stakeholders recognize, value, admire, and even love.[9]

Connectedness: Stakeholder engagement and partnerships

TVC companies are well aware of the external world and their stakeholders. They move away from merely seeing the so-called *primary* stakeholders of investors, employees, suppliers and customers, to *recognizing* secondary *or* indirect *stakeholders* such as local communities, governments, NGOs, society and the planet at large. It is this threshold that differentiates the TVC approach from earlier stages of sustainability.

TVC companies excel at stakeholder engagement – an expression of the principle of connectedness. They hold dialogues at different levels of the organization.

The new understanding of organizations is a living network in which collective value is generated by human connectedness, co-creativity and a sense of common purpose. Sustainability performance is a function of cocreating value with multiple stakeholders in a dynamic web and interconnected and interdependent relationships.

Thus, there is an important role for what is defined as "collective leadership" with a focus on building partnerships within a dynamic value-creation network, both inside and outside the firm. This will need to be based on an authentically shared vision toward solving shared societal issues. Ultimately, at this state, interacting with stakeholders becomes a reciprocal, co-creative and regenerative "win-together" process.

Organization: Chobani yoghurt

Chobani was founded in 2005 by Turkish–Kurdish businessman Hamdi Ulukaya.

Chobani was inspired by Ulukaya's childhood raising sheep and goats and making cheese with his family. Not impressed by the yoghurt options available in the United States, Ulukaya made strained yoghurt at his home in Upstate New York, where he had moved from Turkey to study English at the age of 22. In 2005, after seeing an ad for a former Kraft Foods yoghurt plant for sale, Ulukaya bought it with a small loan from the US small business fund.

He launched the strained yoghurt business with the help of a handful of the plant's former employees. His initial goal was to provide consumers with a more authentic, nutritious and accessible yoghurt. In less than five years after launch, it became the leading seller of Greek yoghurt in America. Since then, the company has been expanding tastes to win a greater share in the overall yoghurt category. The company employs more than 2,000 staff and generates more than $1.5 billion in revenue annually.

But for CEO Hamdi Ulukaya, the rapid and huge business success of Chobani did not distract him from his original goals. First, he wanted to create a healthy product for consumers and for the planet. Chobani yoghurt is made without any preservatives or artificial flavors/colors and does not use milk from cows treated with growth hormones. Second, he wanted to take care of the workers who make it and the communities that they were part of. In 2016, he rewarded his employees with millions in shares, making some of the company's longest-serving employees become millionaires.

Chobani is also bringing back jobs to communities: one-third of Chobani's employees are legally resettled refugees and immigrants.

For Ulukaya, all this is part of the purpose of business: since governments aren't solving problems like the income gap and the refugee crisis on their own, corporations should. He stated that "Companies should focus on humanity and not just on their bottom lines: Business is still the strongest, most effective way to change the world".[10]

Creating these stakeholder benefits were an end in themselves, rather than a means to create shareholder benefit. Hamdi Ulukaya pursued a shared purpose of serving society by growing his business. This makes the company a good example of TVC: value is created for (1) society – by supporting refugees, poor communities, sustainable production and community entrepreneurship, (2) its clients – by providing healthy and tasty products and (3) its own people – by providing work and co-ownership.

Another feature of TVC companies is that they built *stakeholder coalitions* in order to tackle a shared complex problem. For example, under the commitment to meet Paris Agreement targets ten years early, by 2040, many companies have joined the Climate Pledge.[11] Companies from diverse sectors, including direct competitors, are collaborating in tackling climate change through comprehensive and measurable interventions on emissions. Similarly, seven international nonprofit organizations created the "We Mean Business" coalition, which has the mission of "working with the world's most influential businesses to take to drive policy ambition and accelerate the transition to a zero-carbon economy".[12] There are similar global coalitions working on SDGs-related issues, such as sustainable food and agriculture, fashion, forestry and fishery.

We can also recognize a TVC mindset in what is known as *corporate activism*, a trend we have witnessed in the last decade. In 2017 the outdoor apparel company Patagonia demonstrated that its mission to "save the planet" is not merely a nice slogan. Patagonia sued the US President Trump after he decided to cut the funding for nature reserves and monuments – and this court case is still pending. And in 2019, Patagonia closed down its offices so that employees could join a strike alongside youth climate activists. "Business has to pick up the mantle when government fails you", said Patagonia CEO Rose Marcario, describing this trend of corporate activism.[13]

Ice cream company Ben & Jerry's is another example of this trend. In June 2020, when the unarmed black man George Floyd was killed at the hands of white police officers, and protests against racial injustice spread all over the world, the ice cream maker called on consumers to "dismantle white supremacy" and "grapple with the sins of our past". "What happened to George Floyd was not the result of a bad apple; it was the predictable consequence of a racist and prejudiced system and culture that has treated Black bodies as the enemy from the beginning", said the spokesperson of the company.[14] In the days that followed, companies such as Nike, Netflix, Twitter, Disney, Facebook, Starbucks and Intel followed Ben & Jerry's example by condemning racism and injustice.

This is a watershed moment in the corporate world; this was unheard of under the Growth Triangle. Until very recently, champions of the shareholder primacy model would argue that corporations are not designed for making public policy. Their idea was that "political" initiatives are contrary to the creation of shareholder value and should be avoided by management. But it is now evident corporate activists have put that logic upside down: brands with a societal purpose don't lose but *generate value* in a world where conscious consumers vote with their wallets.

This trend raises the bar on business sustainability. There is in fact a distinct business logic behind the approach to value creation taken by these visionary companies. They recognize the strategic alignment of the needs of society, their customers and themselves. Because these needs can be aligned, the firm can develop an aligned value creation strategy, serving these needs simultaneously. This alignment can be depicted in the model of Figure 5.3, the TVC Marshmallow model.

The TVC Marshmallow model can be used to achieve alignment between the various objectives of the business. If this alignment is neglected, companies can be accused of *greenwashing*. This fate befell British bank HSBC in 2021 when a group of investors worth $2.4 trillion suspected the bank of greenwashing as it continues to fund coal projects despite pledging to obtain carbon neutrality. They want the bank to reduce its funding of fossil fuel-based assets.[15]

This is the new battleground for reputation management: how sincere are companies in tackling social and environmental issues and how can they back this up with consistent action?

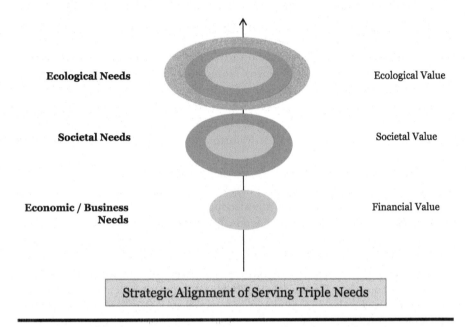

Ecological Needs   Ecological Value

Societal Needs   Societal Value

Economic / Business   Financial Value
Needs

Strategic Alignment of Serving Triple Needs

Figure 5.3 Triple Value Marshmallow model

Competence: Product and market innovation

The opportunity for TVC arises when companies discover what societal issues are strategically relevant to the organization and to what extent these issues could actually present new opportunities for growth. When companies find the intersection between social needs and the market opportunity that this can provide, they can make the next step: to make the strategic choice to apply their distinctive company assets to solving these social challenges. With company assets, we don't merely mean their capital but also their human resources and technology; they represent the competitive capacity of the firm.

If they do so successfully, these companies will have found the "sweet spot" of sustainable value creation.

Value creation is not an on-off transaction, but a dynamic process in a dynamic web of value chain partners – the value system – which allows stakeholders to co-create value together.[16] The co-creative nature of this relationship allows for markets to becoming testing grounds for *product innovation*. Many companies are actually engaging their customers on open source innovation platforms. Sustainability challenges can be used as an opportunity to expand the company's market.

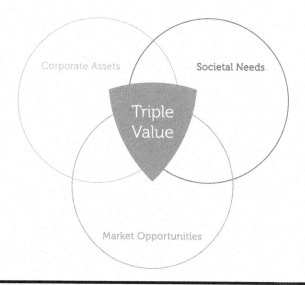

Figure 5.4 The Triple Value sweetspot

Organization: Impossible food

Stanford Biochemistry professor Patrick Brown took an 18-month sabbatical in which he researched how to overcome the negative effects of intensive animal farming. In 2011 he established the company Impossible Food solely dedicated to offering plant-based meat.[17] Their signature product is a plant-based "Impossible Burger" that tastes exactly as a meat-based burger but that also has a net-positive impact on human health, animal well-being and the environment. The Impossible Burger is a gluten-free, plant-based meat made from soy and potato protein. It uses 95% less land, 74% less water, 87% less greenhouses than an ordinary meat burger.[18] Yet it is also run as a profitable business. The Oakland, California-based brand, which has raised $1.3 billion since its inception in 2011, is now valued at $2 billion.[19] In the process, the problems associated with intensive meat-based farming have been turn in an enormous growth market. Data released in March 2020 shows that sales of plant-based foods that directly replace animal products have grown 29% in the past two years to $5 billion.[20]

Mainstream burger chains (like Honest Burgers, Byron Burgers etc.) now have meat-free burgers, and quite often they charge *more* for the plant-based burger than the beef one – an indicator, perhaps, of future demand trends (even though the true costs are less!).

Effectively, Impossible Burger aligned the needs of the planet (lowering carbon emissions from meat production), society (health of people), the consumer (tasty food), as well as the company itself (profitable product). This example of creating an alternative to the meat industry demonstrates the generative power of markets.

The example of Impossible Food illustrates – true to its name – that nothing is impossible. Companies can reconceive planetary and societal problems, as unmet market needs that the company is related to, and thus reframe these needs as *the growth markets of tomorrow*. As we have seen, this is not just marketing rhetoric: it is in line with the principle of markets as generative relationships, through which companies can evolve and innovate in co-creation with their customers.

Creativity: Vision and goals

TVC companies have a strong creative quality: they aim to create new products and new markets to solve issues that have not yet been solved before. Thus, TVC approach is not about *sharing* the value already created by firms, which is the traditional redistribution approach underlying the notions of corporate philanthropy and CSR. Rather, they show that it is about *creating* and thus *expanding* the pool of economic and human/societal value. In other words, the firm's value creation capacity has been enhanced.

This creative capacity is unleashed when companies set *positive impact goals*, which are both visionary and realizable. Goals should be inspiring and compelling, so that everyone wants to follow and goals become collective goals. So they go beyond short-term performance targets and look at the long term. However, if the vision is too far away and the goals are open-ended, people will find it difficult to enact on it. Ideally, in TVC companies the goal setting is a collective process, so as to ensure optimal engagement.

TVC companies are prepared *to be held accountable* externally for their societal purpose. For example, they are voluntarily subscribing to international frameworks of the SDGs, the Paris Climate Agreement and the EU Green Deal. In fact, TVC companies practice what they preach: they proactively lobby with the government not *against* but *in favor* of taxes and regulations that support the transition to sustainability, thus creating a level playing field for all market players, and they precompetitively address issues that affect the common good.

This attitude is also demonstrated by the *ownership and governance structures* of the firm; this should be representative of its stakeholder field, fully inclusive and gender balanced. In these companies, executive compensation is measured against sustainability principles and collective impact targets, rather than merely financial targets and stock price that tend to undermine connectedness and creativity within the firm.

Organization: Royal DSM – malnutrition

Royal DSM is a Dutch multinational active in the fields of life science and nutrition. On top of strong and consistent profits over many years, DSM has been among the leaders in the annual Dow Jones Sustainability

Index.[21] Our research showed that DSM presents a clear example of the TVC approach.

DSM started out in 1902 as the Dutch State Mines (hence the acronym DSM), but when the last coal mines closed in the 1970s, the firm embarked on a process of transformation continuing up to today. Evidently, DSM has displayed a high degree of *context awareness* in its evolution. It first diversified into the (petro) chemicals field, and later into essential nutrients such as synthetic vitamins and other ingredients for the feed, food and pharmaceutical industries.

The most recent wave of transformation was initiated by Feike Sijbesma, DSM's CEO, after witnessing poverty firsthand on a trip to Africa. Exploring the market needs in Africa, he realized that improving nutrition in developing countries is fundamental to breaking the cycle of poverty. More specifically, it is necessary to provide the right nutrients to pregnant women and their infants. Optimizing the quality of nutrition during a critical 1,000-day window of opportunity from conception until a child reaches two years of age has a dramatic impact on its physical and cognitive development, and substantially improves the child's future prospects.

Impressed by the needs of masses of undernourished people, Sijbesma and his team realized that this was a market opportunity for DSM, as the firm was an expert in nutrients and other food ingredients. This insight helped the company to reposition itself as a leader in combatting malnutrition. In doing so, they expanded the mission of DSM: "As the world's leading producer of micronutrients including vitamins, DSM is taking its responsibility to help solve the world's greatest solvable problem: malnutrition, affecting 2 billion people across the globe".[22]

Sijbesma believed that investing in nutrition can not only break the cycle of poverty and build thriving societies and markets, but can also benefit the business objectives of DSM by developing a new market. By establishing partnerships with UN's World Food Program, which is a sign of *connectedness*, DSM turned a global problem into a business growth opportunity of enormous scale. As a business, DSM committed itself to achieving very tangible goals: to reach 50 million beneficiaries (pregnant and lactating women and children under two) by 2030. This demonstrates the firm's *creativity* and *competence*.

To show that these objectives are not merely window dressing to boost DSM's sustainable profile, the firm's management board linked its remuneration and executive bonus to DSM's social/environmental performance.[23] These bold steps had an interesting side effect, as a senior DSM executive told us: "Our real commitment to societal goals is inspiring our own people. Since taking on fighting malnutrition as part of our mission, our employee engagement has grown substantially. It encourages people to bring their whole selves into their job".

In summary, this case shows that TVC has tangible benefits for society, markets and the organization's employees.

Organizational capabilities

The above business practices can be translated into organizational capabilities that TVC companies will need to cultivate. As business scholar Henry Mintzberg observed: "Organization capabilities are critical yet intangible assets that cannot be duplicated. These assets matter more than any other when implementing strategy, yet we often do not plan for them as meticulously as other physical or financial assets".[24] Organizational capabilities become critical if we want transition to a higher level of sustainability performance.

How can these capabilities be developed? Organizational capabilities are the collective mindsets, qualities and competencies of the people in your company. It requires leadership to develop these critical assets. This is the subject of Part 3 of this book, where we will look at leadership competencies required for TVC.

Let's now first explore the outlines of a TVC model, so that we can keep track of the various steps (and cracks) in the causal chain from leadership and organizational capabilities to actually generating positive impact for society and the planet.

Notes

1 Porter, M., & Kramer, M. (2011). The big idea: Creating shared value. *Harvard Business Review* (January/February 2011).
2 Senge, P. (1990). *The Fifth Discipline – the Art and Practice of the Learning Organization.* New York: Doubleday/Currency.
3 Interview on Dutch television Tegenlicht; and www.duurzaambedrijfsleven.nl/agri-food/32283/ceo-carlsberg
4 www.patagonia.com/company-info.html.
5 www.salesforce.com/news/stories/how-far-can-the-1-1-1-model-go-this-tech-darling-has-a-unique-approach/.
6 Polman, P. (2011). www.forumforthefuture.org/blog/six-ways-unilever-has-achieved-success-through-sustainability-and-how-your-business-can-too.
7 https://globescan.com/unilever-patagonia-ikea-sustainability-leadership-2019/.
8 www.patagonia.com/company-info.html.
9 Sisodia, R., Wolfe, D., & Sheth, J. (2007). *Firms of Endearment.* Wharton, TX: Wharton School publication.
10 Real Leaders (2016). Retrieved from: https://real-leaders.com/hamdi-ulukaya-the-turkish-muslim-who-just-made-americans-richer/.
11 www.theclimatepledge.com.

12 www.wemeanbusinesscoalition.org.

13 *Time* Magazine, September 23, 2019. https://time.com/5684011/patagonia/.

14 https://edition.cnn.com/2020/06/03/business/ben--jerrys-george-floyd/index.html.

15 www.forbes.com/sites/oliverwilliams1/2021/01/10/europes-largest-bank-suspected-of-greenwashing/?sh=67ffaf5a5e8c.

16 Scott, W.R., & Davis, G. F. (2007). *Organizations, Rational and Open Systems.* New York: Taylor & Francis.

17 https://psmag.com/news/the-biography-of-a-plant-based-burger#.1dzfvzx4b.

18 https://brightvibes.com/544/en/the-science-behind-the-impossible-burger.

19 www.reuters.com/article/us-impossible-foods-fundraising-exclusiv-idUSKCN 1SJ0YK.

20 www.gfi.org/marketresearch.

21 "DSM ranks high in annual Dow Jones Sustainability Index", Biofuels Digest, retrieved from: www.biofuelsdigest.com/bdigest/2015/09/13/dsm-klm-rank-high-in-annual-dow-jones-sustainability-index/.

22 Comments Feike Sijbesma, retrieved from www.dsm.com/corporate/sustainability/nutrition.html.

23 Kolk, A., & Perego, P. (January 2014) Sustainable bonuses: Sign of corporate responsibility or window dressing? *Journal of Business Ethics, 119*(1), 1–15.

24 Dynamic capabilities are more important for success than strategy. Mintzberg, H., Ahlstrand, B., & Lampel, J. (1998). *Strategy Safari: A Guided Tour through the Wilds of Strategic Management.* New York: Prentice-Hall.

Chapter 6

The Triple Value creation measurement model

You can only manage what you can measure – this applies to Triple Value too. The review of the emerging business practices of leading sustainability companies can help us conceive of a new and expanded value creation measurement model. This is still an emerging concept as these companies set both new goals and employ new methods as to how to achieve them, but it greatly helps to create some order in the apparent chaos of change.

The new model, which can also be defined as a new "theory of change", will be a useful tool for business leadership: it will provide clarity that leaders need to deal with the complexity inherent in sustainable value creation for multiple stakeholders. The new model will shed light on the entire chain of cause and effect, incorporating human agency as an additional input factor, as well as accounting for indirect and unintended effects as outcome and impact. This new model will reveal opportunities for identifying the value drivers for Triple Value creation.

The need for new measurement models

"We should reinvent capitalism by internalizing all externalities", says Peter Bakker, executive director of the World Business Council for Sustainable Development (WBCSD).[1]

Indeed, Triple Value creation (TVC) will not happen if companies continue to use conventional economic indicators as measures of their performance, be it at a corporate or project level. Conventional indicators tend to merely measure financial results and not the value created with the different stakeholders. Moreover, most financial output indicators tend to misrepresent the real cost price for the value created or destroyed.

Equating the creation of value with the generation of financial output is like confusing the goal with the goalposts – mixing up the means with the end. Organizations that do that, for example by focusing on maximizing short-term profits for their own needs, may end up destroying social value and being accused of greenwashing. Footwear company, Puma, recognized the danger of this approach and created an environmental profit and loss, accounting for impacts on water supplies from its production process.[2] Even though this was done on an experimental basis, it underscores the need to "change the rules of the current game". The basic logic is: *you can only manage what you measure.*

Therefore, TVC will require that companies adopt *integrated performance measurement* systems, with its own KPIs. Obviously, short-term profits and revenues remain important, but TVC companies realize that they *are just indicators.* They represent the milestones along the road, but they don't determine the destination.

In traditional companies, value creation models are typically used by finance departments, aimed at retroactively measuring results. In TVC companies, however, measurement systems are used to ensure that its sustainable strategy execution is on target and that progress is made along the way. In these companies, the measurement systems are used to support the execution of a forward-looking strategy by creating feedback loops for holding executives accountable, as well as for collective learning and development.

Expanding the chain of cause and effect

There are many conceptual models and theories of change in economics to explain how organizations create value. However – as we discussed – the current models tend to be rather limited, because they generally focus only on direct inputs (such as capital, material resources and human labor) and direct outputs (such as number of products or services sold and financial results like return on equity, profit and revenue).

This is the common action logic of the Growth Triangle, depicted in Figure 6.1. The trouble is that there are not only *direct and intended* causes and effects of business activity, as the Growth Triangle assumes. Obviously, as the climate emergency is

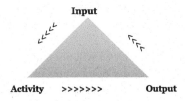

Figure 6.1 The Growth Triangle

showing us, there are also *indirect* and *unintended* causes and effects that can stay hidden for a long time, but that are important for the sustainability of humanity and the planet, and which have an (negative) impact on value creation.

"There is no sustainability without transparency", said Volkert Engelsman, CEO of Eosta, which works on rewarding organic growers for their ecosystem services through full costs accounting in the supply chain. "There is no free trade as long as we externalize costs on nature and suppliers", he said.[3]

There are models that do capture the long term and indirect effects of business and therefore provide a more complete and accurate map for value creation. For example, in the context of sustainability it is increasingly common to use the "result framework" (also called "logical framework") that is used in program evaluations to assess the relationship to progress in achieving results. It helps to achieve strategic objectives of large policy projects and programs.[4]

We will use the basic terminology of this framework in the following discussion.

From output to impact

We can first look at the "output" side. When a company has sold a product to a customer, this is considered as *output* (and likewise the revenue received falls into this category). But, in reality, the causal chain does not stop here – there are other (in) direct results. The customer will *do* things with the product. He or she will consume the product, with the expectation of an effect. So there is a particular action followed by another effect. For example, a parent may buy a product with nutritional value for his child. The consumer expects that this product will have a measurable positive effect on the health of the child, although it may take a while to determine its full effect. This effect is defined as *outcome*.

Then, the outcome will have further aggregate effects on a societal and planetary level, which is called *impact*, which can be positive, neutral and/or negative and intended or unintended. Impacts are the indirect and long-term effects of outcomes. While outcomes can be correlated to the company's output, impact can only be contributed to by the firm – there are other causes necessary to create impact.

To build on the earlier example, if all children experience the positive effects from the food product, the product (and thus the producer) will contribute to the improvement of the health of a nation and world community. Likewise, if we help shifting the production and consumption from animal-based proteins to plant-based proteins, our efforts will contribute to a more sustainable agriculture and food system, as well as a positive effect on the global climate.

While outputs are visible as soon as the activities that created them have been completed, outcomes generally manifest at a later point in time. In an even longer term, and on a wider scale, the activities can have an impact on communities, society and environment. Such an impact can be both intended or unintended, and both positive or negative, or a mixture of those.

We should stress here that, on the one hand, it can take time to move from decisions to outputs, outcomes and finally impact at the social/environmental level (and this needs to be factored in), it's also possible to have a significant impact in a short space of time. For instance, when leaders of the manufacturing industry stop using plastic packaging on all their products with immediate effect, this has a pro-environmental effect rapidly. This should be stressed because we don't want to reinforce the common (misguided) assumption that sustainability change *always* takes a long time to work through.

> Leadership reflection: What impact on society and the environment could my organization have in the next three months? What about the next three years? And what over the next ten years?

Human agency and leadership

From a whole human being and interdependent living systems viewpoint, we also need to expand the "input" side of the results framework. Input typically includes items such as capital, skilled labor, raw materials, ecosystem resources like water and also intellectual property. Yet a critical piece of input is missing: the mind of the actors in the cause and effects chain, especially the mindsets of the leaders and managers. The question of what mindset we adopt and cultivate is a very real one – as we will discuss in the next section of the book.

From a systems viewpoint, this omission makes no sense, particularly when indirect effects such as impact are considered. How can you determine the desired societal and planetary impact without the concordant view and intentions of the leaders? How can you realize a vision without first visualizing it? The future can only be created with the future in mind.

We need to put human agency back in the causal chain of value creation. In fact, it should be the place where the causal chain begins – this is the role of leadership. The human mind is a critical additional causal factor in the chain of cause and effect. Impact and human agency belong together: while net positive impact can only be created by conscious effort, it would be impossible to create net positive impact without human agency. With human agency, we can extend the causal chain into the future to account for long-term direct and indirect effects. This can also help to make leaders more accountable for their (non) actions.

As Peter Bakker, executive director of the WBCSD, says:

> It is a good step that most companies now report on their negative social and environmental impact, but this means nothing if they don't have operational plans to back this up. We should hold company boards accountable for having and executing these plans.[5]

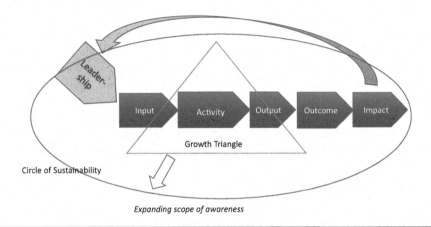

Figure 6.2 Triple Value measurement model

Now we can put together a more complete version of the logical framework in which the process of value creation spans leaders, organizations, markets and society.

While this model seems to be linear (hence the word *value chain*), it is actually holistic and circular in nature as it is meant to represent the entire *value system*, with multiple feedback loops. For example, leadership does not only lie at the root of converting stakeholder needs into inputs, but it also spans the entire value creation model. Leadership can help to ensure that activity could also be socially appropriate (e.g. no slavery) rather than just staying within planetary boundaries, and it can translate output into impact (e.g., through sustainable marketing).

The main benefit of this model is that it can help leaders of companies that aspire to be sustainable to more clearly define the positive systems impact that they wish to have, by linking business objectives to specific market (consumer) outcomes and societal needs that they bear an impact on. In this context, the UN SDGs will be useful in representing an overarching framework of goals, which we will need to achieve in order to maintain a sustainable society on this planet. Indeed, many leading companies are aligning their impact objectives to the SDGs.[6]

Organization: Siemens – Business to Society (B2S)

Traditionally, value creation is defined in terms of a company creating perceived benefit to the individual customer (B2C) or benefit to a fellow company (B2B). However, in the TVC approach the focus is not on creating customer/company benefit (outcome) but benefit for the customer/company *as well as* the society and environment (impact).

The German company Siemens AG calls this approach Business to Society (B2S). "It's all about people", says Joe Kaeser, CEO of Siemens. "And it's all about people because it's all about society. It's about the societal purpose a company gives to".[7] As Siemens defines itself as a B2S company, it claims to focus on leveraging all of its assets, talents and partnerships to have a positive social impact everywhere that it operates. This includes enabling local economic growth and job creation, reducing greenhouse gas emissions, and including more women and minorities in the workplace, says the firm.

"A company has to have a purpose and that purpose has to be creating value for society. A company which does not serve society should not exist", says Kaeser.

From Triple Needs to Triple Value

The TVC measurement model comprises all the crucial steps in the value creation system, not just the input–activity–output chain of the Growth Triangle. It is as if we have opened the curtains so that we can see the entire value system context.

By virtue of its holistic nature, the model can help to connect the respective needs of the business (output), customers (outcome) and society (impact), with the value creation capacity of leaders, employees and suppliers – which make up an expanded version of input. In short, it will align serving "Triple Needs" with creating "Triple Value".

Now that we have conceived of a comprehensive value creation model which has restored human agency and leadership to the rightful place at the foundation of the creative process, it is time to look at what sort of leadership is needed for Triple Value creation.

System: TVC versus greenwashing

The TVC measurement approach should incorporate both the benefits and harms to society and the environment by the way business is done. The TVC model not only encompasses the positive and negative aspects of value in the stakeholder network but also accounts for conflicting values, that is, where one stakeholder benefit may create a negative effect for another stakeholder. This can be done, for example, through the value-mapping model of Nancy Bocken and her colleagues, which distinguishes value created, value delivered and value captures.[8] This sets TVC companies apart from those who claim to serve society but are actually engaged in delivering benefits and value to customers alone, and so are "green washing" their reputation.

For instance, Facebook claims that its mission is to solve a social problem by "bringing people closer together". Yet social psychologists' research suggests the (social) well-being of using platforms like this is far from entirely positive. Addiction to social media causes considerable harm to society. The same greenwashing applies to Uber, which claims to serve society by "bringing transportation for everyone, everywhere", while failing to provide fair wages for their drivers. The value they provide to their customers may be high (comfort, speed, low prize, etc.), but the negative effects on society (low wages, unemployment, etc.) have been overlooked.

Notes

1 Bakker, P. webinar Driving System Change, May 25, 2021.
2 Nidumolu, R., Kramer, K., & Zeitz, J. (2012). Connecting heart to head: A framework for sustainable growth. *Stanford Social Innovation Review*, Winter. Retrieved from: www.ssireview.org/articles/entry/connecting_heart_to_head.
3 Interview.
4 OECD 2010; Independent Evaluation Group of the World Bank (2020), retrieved from www.oecd.org/dac/peer-reviews/World Bank. Independent Evaluation Group.
5 Bakker, P. webinar Driving System Change, May 25, 2021.
6 See for example de SDG Sector Roadmaps defined by WBCSD: www.wbcsd.org/ Programs/People-and-Society/Sustainable-Development-Goals/SDG-Sector-Roadmaps.
7 www.future-of-leadership.org/how-to-give-a-purpose-to-your-company/.
8 Bocken, N., Short, S., Rana, S., & Evans, S. (2013). A value mapping tool for sustainable business modelling. *Corporate Governance*, *13*(5), 482–497. DOI: 10.1108/ CG-06-2013-0078.

Part 3

How?

How can leaders execute the new
value creation approach?

Chapter 7

Leadership – how to develop the sustainability mindset

In this chapter we will explore the important role of leadership in shifting organizations towards TVC, looking especially at the level of the underlying leadership mindsets, a function of "self leadership" that ultimately drives TVC leadership. By reviewing breakthroughs in the science of the mind and our understanding of human intelligence, we will construct a whole-brain map encapsulating our full human potential. This can serve as building blocks for a new TVC leadership mindset model.

The important role of leadership

We observed that leading organizations adjust to the new reality of sustainability and the underlying principle of interconnectedness exactly *because of their leadership*. It is the company's leadership that perceives the changing environment, comprehends the significance of these changes and subsequently takes measures to change the organization accordingly. This specifically applies to TVC organizations. They are demonstrating TVC capabilities, because their leadership possesses specific qualities to do so.

As we have seen in previous chapters, these qualities require a high degree of systems awareness to recognize the sustainability shifts we are experiencing. In particular, we need an "outside in" perspective allowing us to move from the Growth Triangle to the Circle of Sustainability, while solving overcoming resistance and obstacles on the way.

DOI: 10.4324/9781003119302-11

Obviously, these unique TVC qualities don't come out of anywhere: they need to be created. Throughout history, we have seen leaders with outstanding systems leadership qualities: people who changed the larger societal and economic systems, and they have been extensively studied.

For example, leaders such as Mahatma Gandhi or Nelson Mandela demonstrated exceptional degrees of systems leadership to change at the level of the system, while also excelling at the level of self and their relationships. James Macgregor Burns, who studied these world leaders, defined their style as 'transformational leadership", as distinct from transactional leadership.[1] While the transactional leadership refers to skills and knowledge aimed at making people work effectively within the current status quo, Burns described transformational leadership as a process in which leaders and followers help each other to transforming the status quo, so as to meet unmet social needs.[2]

Robert Greenleaf observed that a similar people-oriented leadership style, which focused on igniting the intrinsic motivation of employees, was leading to success in companies such as AT&T. He described it as "'servant leadership', emphasizing the need for the leader to put him-/herself in the service of others".[3] These schools of leadership focus less on personal traits and more on contextual and adaptive dynamics in relation to the needs of the followers. Likewise, less attention is paid to the top leader, but more to the phenomena of *leadership*, which can be demonstrated by one or more people in a decentralized, shared and distributed manner.

Obviously, with its focus on the context and changing the status quo, TVC leadership builds on these schools of leadership. But we believe that TVC leadership also goes beyond them as it is specifically aimed at sustainability at all levels of the system – SOS – which means that on top of outer systems we see ourselves and our organization as well. A number of contemporary business leaders allude to this.

Bill George, the former CEO of Medtronics, explained:

> The leaders that we need in the future – compassionate authentic leaders – are quite different from the past decades. They have an intrinsic motivation to contribute to the welfare of others. It comes from the inside not from some sort of external reward. They lead not just with the intellect, but with the whole person in a holistic form of leadership.[4]

Paul Polman, who turned Unilever into the globally most respected sustainable company, said:

> You need a firm belief in the core responsibility of solving these challenges yourself, and not delegating that to someone else. If you don't have that inside of you, then we can all sit here and be critical about government and legislation, but where are you in this? You cannot be a bystander in the system that gives you life in the first place.[5]

Volkert Engelsman, CEO of Eosta, an organic wholesaler, summed it up as follows:

> This is the first time in history that we are exceeding the carrying capacity of the planet. So it is also the first time that business leaders will need to take the health of the planet into account in their decision making.[6]

According to Engelsman, this type of leadership is still extremely rare. "This is not something we learn at business schools. Instead, this has to come from our own humanity, our innate wisdom". With Engelsman, we believe that this is the new frontier in business leadership.

Leadership reflection

How can I lead with my "innate wisdom"? What does holistic leadership mean for me, relative to how I am leading right now? Do I take full responsibility for all sustainability challenges? Do I bring in my full heart for all stakeholders? To what degree (and where) am I a bystander?

Science: *Homo sapiens* – leadership DNA

Modern research suggests that the call for contextual leadership is not so much a "new phase" of leadership, but the resurfacing of leadership behavior that is aligned to natural human needs and qualities. Anthropologists tend to agree that this contextual leadership may be the most natural style because it suits our particular make up as *Homo sapiens*.[7] For 300,000 years, our ancestors lived as hunter-gatherers in groups of some 150 people, loosely connected to larger tribes. They survived by virtue of their decentralized and adaptive leadership styles, exhibited equally by men and women, allowing them to flexibly deal with changing environments and collaborate with other groups as needed.

With the advent of the agricultural revolution around 11,000 BCE, the hunter-gatherers settled down in communities with land holdings to grow crops, a new leadership style emerged with a top-down orientation aimed at protecting its assets, mostly held by men.[8] It is this masculine style that evolved into the military leadership of the colonial era and the machine-like leadership of the industrial revolution, only to be countered in recent decades by a call for leadership that is more democratic, egalitarian, gender-balanced and responsive to societal and ecological issues.

Many of us believe, however, that top-down leadership styles are a dominant part of human nature. This is simply not looking deeply enough into history. Science has indicated that this more humane, caring and context-sensitive leadership potential is innate to the human mind. Our brains are wired this way. In this sense, the contextual leadership style is more natural. In any event, it seems to fit better with the present call for more democratic and egalitarian leadership that is capable of dealing with the late contextual challenge of sustainability.

The biologist E.O. Wilson said: "Only in the last moment in history, has the delusion arisen that people can flourish apart from the rest of the world".[9]

Organizations: Executive search firms are looking for new types of leaders

Leading an organization seems difficult enough in these challenging times. For CEOs to make sure that you meet your targets, adjust to new technologies, create new products and motivate your people – this list is long. And now leaders are asked to lead through complexity and create societal benefit *on top of* business performance?

Yes, this is in fact what the recruiters of top executives are looking for. Global search firm Egon Zehnder evaluates the leaders of the future on the basis of the "transformational leadership model", which lists "anchoring in society ..." as one of the five features of leadership. Egon Zehnder partner Friedrich Kuhn, who helped design Egon Zehnder's transformational leadership model, told us:

> We are looking for CEO's who are capable of transitioning from "leading organizations" to "leading with your organization in society". This is not an easy task – we are still trying to understand how to help leaders in this transition, which entails a major increase in awareness and empathy – but the trend is inevitable and irrevocable.[10]

These words are echoed by another global executive search firm, Russell Reynolds, who looked into developing a leadership model suitable for the times of today. Clarke Murphy, CEO of Russell Reynolds, said:

> For transformation at the level and scale needed, organizations need to focus on making sustainability sustainable. This is more than a matter of strategy, policy and process – it is fundamentally about leadership and people. Leaders on boards and in the C-suite have a huge opportunity to make sustainability central to their organization's culture and leadership.[11]

Russell Reynolds joined up with the United Nations Global Compact to investigate how this gap in the executive search market could be filled. How can leaders and organizations make sustainability core to their DNA? They concluded that what's most needed are leaders with a "sustainable mindset", which they defined as follows: "The belief that business is not a commercial activity divorced from the wider societal and environmental context in which it operates".[12]

It starts with self-leadership

The question is: how can we cultivate this type of leadership? The practice of changing our mindsets starts with self-leadership. We have to look inward at our own mindsets and beliefs. It is on this basis that we can build the outer systems leadership required for sustainability. Erica Fox, author and executive coach, writes, "Once you change your mindset, you'll change your awareness, which will lead to new attitudes and new behaviour, which will impact your colleagues, others around you and ultimately the world".[13]

This brings us to a deeper analysis of shifting mindsets. Mindsets refer to interior patterns of mind, mental models or frames of reference.[14] The mindset of leaders determines how they see the world, how they reason and how they make meaning and behave in response to their experiences in the world. In essence, the mindsets determine the scope and capacity of leadership for positive change.

Importantly, mindsets can be trained and cultivated by individuals, which provide us with a necessary agency to enact change. One way of understanding mindsets is through the lens of values. While mindsets tend to be somewhat "implicit" and hidden to the consciousness, values can be made "explicit" by asking people to indicate "what is of value?" or "what is important?" In a sense, values are attributes of the underlying mindset. However, in the context of sustainability, we are confronted with many conflicting values – for example, short-term stability versus disruptive innovation necessary for the long term – which we can't effectively address by merely asking questions.

So we will have to look at our mind more deeply. This is really a question about the potential of our mind: can we awaken qualities of mind that are still hidden?

Sheri Flies, CEO Costco, is hopeful that we can: "This is really about the next level of human development. If all of us were able to get to the highest in ourselves, we'd be able to see through these problems."[15]

The discovery of the mind: A new perspective on leadership development

For centuries, the mind – our awareness or consciousness – has been a "black box" of science.[16] Psychiatrist Iain McGilchrist makes the point that the mind is the one thing that can be experienced from the inside, but not from the outside; while the brain (and the body) can only be seen from the outside, and not from the inside.[17]

This allowed the myth of particular assumptions about the mind – such as the *homo economicus* – to be taken for real and find its center in economic theory.

A recent major breakthrough in neuroscience comes from the discovery that our brains are "plastic", a phenomenon technically known as *neuroplasticity*.[18] Our identity, character and state of mind are not static and fixed – they are a constantly changing and evolving process of moment-to-moment awareness. And we are in charge of the direction in which we evolve; we are not hapless victims of whatever occurs in our mind. Naturally, we suffer from dysfunctional patterns of thinking and varying degrees of pathologies, but this does not mean that the vast majority of us cannot train and develop our mental and emotional capacity.[19]

How does that work? Research has demonstrated that contemplative practices enable people to change their intentions and their behavior. Individuals who practice mindfulness and awareness experience a stronger linkage between intentions and behavior than those who don't engage in these practices. People who take the effort to cultivate the potential of their minds will be able to deal with a complex reality more effectively, recover faster from setbacks, engage with people better and, therefore, generate better results.

The reasons for this is obvious, say researchers Brown and Ryan: "It helps individuals disengage from automatic thoughts and become more open to behavioral change and freedom to make different choices".[20] Rasmus Hougaard and Jacqueline Carter describe this field of mind-training well in their book *The Mind of the Leader*, the importance of which he illustrated with the ancient saying: "Observe your thoughts as they become actions. Observe your actions, as they become habits. And observe your habits as they shape your life".[21]

Leadership example

Marc Benioff, CEO of Salesforce, said:

> One of the best investments I ever made is in my meditation practice. I typically meditate every morning for 30 to 60 minutes. It's a skill that I have used when things have gone wrong in my life. When there are life challenges – whether it was my father's death, health challenges with family members, extreme stress in Salesforce, or worry about the state of the world – I could always find refuge and strength in my meditation practice. This is an investment that has paid off over and over again.[22]

Science: Field of awareness

"I think, therefore I am", wrote Descartes two and half-century ago. But he did not look clearly enough. An important insight from the new mind science (which matches the direct experience of anyone who has attempted to practice

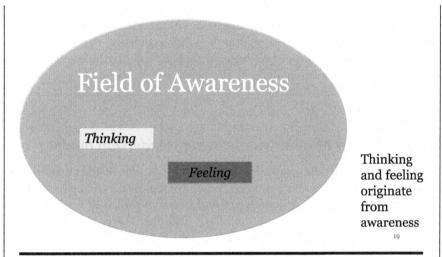

Thinking
and feeling
originate
from
awareness
19

Figure 7.1 Field of awareness

mindfulness) is that the mind is not identical to thinking – thoughts constitute just a part of our consciousness.[23] Thoughts arise *from* our consciousness, our *field of awareness* and subside back into it.

"We are so seduced by thinking and emotion and we don't realize that awareness is at least as powerful of a function. It can hold any emotion, no matter how destructive, any thought, no matter how gigantic", writes renowned meditation teacher Jon Kabat-Zinn.[24]

The field of awareness spans our total experience and provides a constant stream of sensations, feelings and thoughts, with no apparent beginning or end, and no clear shapes and boundaries. Through practices such as mindfulness, the field of awareness can be deepened and expanded, revealing a larger reality of phenomena, both internal and external. You just see and feel more stuff. This enables you and transcends self-limiting categories such as "me", "mine", "us" and "them".

These insights drive a new scientific field of human performance. Just as top-athletes want to perform at their highest possible level, senior executives increasingly train their minds through mindfulness, visualization and linguistic affirmations, on top of training the body, in order to excel at work and life. This can be defined as "awareness-based learning".

Awareness-based learning offers a new gateway into unlocking the mind's full potential. It entails a form of learning that goes beyond cognitive learning (acquiring new *information/knowledge*), which is traditionally taught at school and university. Rather, it cultivates *all human faculties*, including the somatic, emotional, social and spiritual dimensions. It is a form of learning that will unleash our full creative capacity by deepening our awareness of oneself, others, our organizations and the larger systems on which we depend. This may sound abstracts, but it is meant to be a "felt experience" that is induced by practice. In fact, it is the whole brain/whole-body approach to learning that we described in Chapter 3 – indeed, it is the Learner pur sang!

Building blocks of new "whole being" leadership model

Now let's explore what the components are of the new, holistic mindset that we need for systems leadership. In Part 1, we discussed the crucial role of consciousness (and intelligence) in this process.[25] For this part of the book, we will look more deeply at key insights from cognitive science, which is a field that incorporates multidisciplinary viewpoints including brain science.[26]

If the "homo economicus" only represents part of our being, we will need to build a model that represents our whole being. Thus, this model should include all rational, emotional, social and reflective capacities of the human mind. As human beings are living organism, this model should be consistent with six principles of life, making it more complete than the old map rooted in the narrow assumptions of the material paradigm.

What would the full view map look like? To put it in simple terms, if our mind would be a country, on the old map there would be mainly two regions:

1. Thinking – usually attributed to the brain (known as IQ)
2. Manual skills – our physical dimension
   These two match the typical picture of the human being found in economics textbooks, who divided people into rational agents or labor with manual skills.

   Psychologists have known for decades that this is a gross simplification of human nature and human intelligence for that matter – yet it has not sunk into business thinking. Thus, the new map should reveal much more of human nature, going beyond a narrow conception of our capabilities. Again, to use simple terms, it would show four more regions, reflecting other aspects of our being, that are mostly white spots on the current maps used in economics:
3. Our ability to feel, empathize and connect with others. This refers to the field of Emotional and Social Intelligence.[27]
4. Our ability to create, innovate, dream and set long-term goals. Some describe it as creative intelligence.[28]
5. Our capacity to relate with the world, context and systems that we are a part of and that shape our environment. This generally corresponds to what is known as system thinking and systems intelligence.[29]

	Old Map	New Map	6 principles of life
6		Systems Intelligence	Context
5		Consciousness (Awareness)	Consciousness
4		Creative Intelligence	Creativity
3		Emotional Intelligence	Connectedness
2	Manual Skills (Body)	Physical Intelligence	Centeredness
1	Ratio / Intellect (IQ)	Intellect	Competence

Figure 7.2 Levels of intelligence

6. Consciousness – our capacity for cognition, our ability to learn, by developing our mind or consciousness. It corresponds to the ability to cultivate a "growth mindset" instead of a fixed mindset.[30]

The faculties of 5 and 6, context and cognition, respectively, enable us to balance all our internal and external parts, which give rise to our awareness of morality, ethics, intentions and values.[31] With these qualities, we will become better at seeing the whole picture – to seeing things more holistically. This is what we call the *systems mindset*.

It is not too difficult to correlate the six faculties to the six principles of life. The old map faculties correspond to the principle of competence (intellect) and centeredness (our physical existence), while the other four – connectedness, creativity, consciousness and context – can be related to principles of life 3, 4, 5 and 6, respectively.

Taken together, these six faculties expand our map of human potential, which has great implications for leadership and organizations.

The six regions together give us a much better sense of the capacities that are available to us. If regions 1 and 2 would represent the *homo economicus*, regions 1–6 together would represent the *homo sapiens* as we actually are: the conscious human being. This comprehensive map of human capabilities presents more accurately the reality of who we are.

Notes

1 Burns, J. M. (1978). *Leadership*. New York: Harper & Row. See also: Bass, B. M. (1998). *Transformational Leadership: Industrial, Military, and Educational Impact*. Mahwah, NJ: Erlbaum.

2 Ibidem.

3 Greenleaf, R. K., & Spears Larry C. (1982). *Servant Leadership: A journey into the Nature of Legitimate Power and Greatness*. New York: Paulist Press International.

4 Quoted in Tideman, S. G. (2016). *Business as an Instrument of Societal Change – In Conversation with H.H. the Dalai Lama.* Sheffield, UK: Greenleaf Publishing.

5 Confino, J. (October 2, 2013). Interview: Unilever's Paul Polman on diversity, purpose and profits. *The Guardian.* Retrieved from: www.theguardian.com/sustainable-business/unilver-ceo-paul-polman-purpose-profits.

6 Personal Interview.

7 Ferguson, R. B. (2011) *Born to Live: Challenging Killer Myths,* in Sussman, R. and Cloninger, C. R. (eds) *Origin of Altruism and Cooperation,* Springer, pp. 258–259; Fry, D. (2013). *War Peace and Human Nature.* Oxford University Press.

8 Eagly, A. H., & Wood, W. (June 1999). *The Origins of Sex Differences in Human Behavior: Evolved Dispositions Versus Social Roles. American Psychologist,* 54(6), 408–423.

9 Wilson, E. O. (1979). *On Human Nature.* Cambridge, MA: Harvard University Press.

10 Niel Hindle, J. W. (2015). Conversation on Transformational Leadership. Retrieved from www.egonzehnder.com/insight/a-new-leadership-paradigm-for-successful-organizational-transformation.

11 Leadership for the Decade of Action. A United Nations Global Compact-Russell Reynolds Associates study on the characteristics of sustainable business leaders (May 2020). Retrieved from: www.russellreynolds.com/insights/thought-leadership/rra-ungc-unveil-first-of-its-kind-study-sustainable-business-leadership.

12 Ibidem.

13 Fox, E. (2013). *Winning from Within.* New York: Harper Collins.

14 Schein, S. (2015). *A New Psychology for Sustainability Leadership: The Hidden Power of Ecological Worldviews.* Sheffield: Greenleaf Publishing.

15 Quotes in Senge, P. (2008). Necessary Revolution-How Individuals and Organizations are Working together to create a Sustainable World, Bantam Double Day. p. 381.

16 Siegel, D. (2009), *Mindsight; Transform Your Brain with the New Science of Kindness.* New York, NY: Bantam Books; Wallace, B. A. (2007). *Contemplative Science: Where Buddhism and Neuroscience Converge.* New York, NY: Columbia University Press.

17 McGilchrist, I. (October 9, 2009). *The Master and His Emissary: The Divided Brain and the Making of the Western World.* New Haven: Yale University Press.

18 Davidson, R. J., & Begley, S. (2012). *The Emotional Life of Your Brain: How Its Unique Patterns Affect the Way You Think, Feel, and Live, and How You Can Change Them.* New York: Hudson Street Press.

19 Davidson R., & Goleman D. (2018). *The Science of Meditation – How to Change Your Brain, Mind and Body.* Penguin Books.

20 Brown, K. W., & Ryan, R. M. (April 2003). The benefits of being present: Mindfulness and its role in psychological well-being. *Journal of Personality and Social Psychology,* 84(4), 822–848.

21 Hougaard, R., & Carter J. (2018). *The Mind of the Leader: How to Lead Yourself, Your People, and Your Organization for Extraordinary Results.* Harvard, Boston: Harvard Business Press.

22 http://meaningring.com/2019/09/07/life-advice-from-marc-benioff/.

23 In neuroscience the distinction is defined as conceptual awareness (thinking) versus perceptual awareness (direct awareness): Tacikowski, P., Berger, C. C., & Ehrsson, H. H. (July 2017). Dissociating the neural basis of conceptual self-awareness from perceptual awareness and unaware self-processing. *Cerebral Cortex,* 27(7), 3768–3781.

24 https://medium.com/thrive-global/the-father-of-mindfulness-on-what-mindfulness-has-become-ad649c8340cf.

25 Thompson, E. (2007). *Mind in Life: Biology, Phenomenology, and the Sciences of Mind.* Cambridge, MA: Harvard University Press.

26 Davidson, R. J., & Begley, S. (2012). *The Emotional Life of Your Brain: How Its Unique Patterns Affect the Way You Think, Feel, and Live, and How You Can Change Them.* New York: Hudson Street Press.

27 Goleman, D. (1996). *Emotional Intelligence. Why It Can Matter more than IQ.* London: Bloomsberry; Goleman, D. (2007). *Social Intelligence; The New Science of Human Performance.* New York: Random House.

28 Creative intelligence is defined by Nussbaum, B. (2013). *Creative Intelligence: Harnessing the Power to Create, Connect, and Inspire.* Harper Business. He refers to a higher level of intelligence that what we refer to in this context.

29 Senge, P. (1990). *The Fifth Discipline. The Art & Practice of the Learning Organization.* New York: Bantam Double Day; Sharmer, O. (2006). *Theory U – Leading from the Future as it Emerges.* Oakland, USA: Berrett-Koelher.

30 Dweck, C. S. (2006). *Mindset: How You Can Fulfill Your Potential.* London: Robinson; see also: Kahneman, D. (2011). *Thinking Fast and Slow.* New York: Farrar, Straus and Giroux.

31 See for example: Siegel, D. (2009) *Mindsight; Transform Your Brain with the New Science of Kindness.* New York, NY: Bantam Books. Psychologist Laurence Kohlberg speaks of this capacity as highest level of ethics: Kohlberg, L. (1981). *Essays on Moral Development, Vol. I: The Philosophy of Moral Development.* San Francisco, CA: Harper & Row.

Chapter 8

The TVC systems mindset

The TVC mindset has six facets that can be framed in leadership "archetypes", representing qualities of mind that we already possess, but that need to be cultivated in the service of creating sustainable organizations.

The six archetypes are related to six principles of life (Chapter 3), new beliefs we identified in Chapter 4 (the Systems-level) and business practices and organizational competences in Chapter 5 (Organizations), but here we will look specifically at how leaders can apply and practice them (the Self-level).

Nonetheless, given their relatedness at the SOS level, and with a stretch of imagination, the TVC leadership model with its six mindset qualities can be used to counter the six old beliefs that got humanity into trouble, and thus help shift the supertanker of capitalism into a more sustainable direction.

While the old beliefs are distorting our perception of reality, the TVC leadership mindsets sharpen and expand our perception, thus revealing reality more accurately *as it really is*, while illuminating rather than obscuring the problems that we face. In this sense, the practice of TVC Leadership is perhaps the best and historically most opportune strategy toward sustainable systems change. At the very least, it will put you and your organizations firmly into the contest for success in the future that is going to be characterized by more complexity and interconnectedness. By many measures, TVC leadership represents the next level of evolution in business leadership.

We have put the insights of Chapter 7 all together in an integrated framework: a new map for sustainable leadership – which we will call the *TVC leadership mindset model*.

To be consistent with the six principles of life, the TVC leadership mindset model consists of six key qualities. These qualities are innately available to us and have been recognized to some degree in our cultures at earlier times. For that reason we have connected the qualities to familiar leadership archetypes.

Science: Leadership archetypes

In the 1920s, Swiss psychologist Carl Jung attempted to make a holistic map of human consciousness on the basis of working with countless patients. He aimed at helping his patients to integrate various aspects of their mind that had become disintegrated. This led him to develop an integrated theory and define the most common psychological types.[1]

According to Carl Jung, our identity is not limited to one fixed form but instead manifests in various aspects of our mind, including hidden layers of our consciousness, which Jung defined as archetypes. When we identify these (hidden) archetypes, we can learn to integrate them into our identity. Jung defined this as a process of "individuation", enhancing our overall mental health and effectiveness.[2]

Inspired by the work of Jung, author Joseph Campbell observed that the journey of the archetypal hero was found in all the world's myths. Campbell's book *The Hero with Thousands Faces* established the universal applicability of leadership archetypes in the metaphor of the hero's journey.[3]

The pioneering work of Carl Jung inspired a movement of holistic psychotherapy as well as the construction of psychometric models that aim to comprehensively measure human traits and competencies. This has found wide application in the field of management education and leadership development. The MBTI model is perhaps the most well known for this.

We have identified six archetypes that can be used to create a holistic model of TVC leadership, each referring to a particular quality of leadership.

Principles of life	*Qualities of leadership*
Context-relatedness	The Wise
Consciousness	The Learner
Centeredness	The Grounder
Connectedness	The Connector
Competence	The Warrior
Creativity	The Visionary

The first two qualities – the Wise and the Learner – are especially relevant today for adjusting to a more complex interconnected world. We can define them as the *awareness-based systems mindset*, which constitutes a new conceptual approach to leadership. The other four qualities have been more commonly recognized in the leadership literature, but by presenting them as aspects and attributes of the first two qualities, they will take on new significance.

Importantly, the systems dimension will make them suitable to serve as qualities for cultivating the leadership that is needed for the transitioning from the Growth Triangle to the Circle of Sustainability. They are building blocks of a comprehensive TVC leadership model, which – in technical terms – can be characterized as *awareness-based system leadership*. This type of leadership is dedicated to perceiving the systems dimension of reality yet is rooted in the recognition that this springs from our innate awareness.

We will return to this later. Let's first describe the six qualities:

Context awareness: The Wise

Context awareness is the capacity to recognize the rapidly changing context in the world. This centers on the ability to understand and handle increasing levels of complexity, being mindful of paradoxes and dilemmas, while navigating the dynamic interdependence of trends, development and actors in the world.

Some describe this quality as holistic thinking, systems thinking and systems awareness. It comes down to the ability to expand one's perspective and broaden one's view, to grasp trends and developments in the world at large. It also contains the awareness that change is both natural and necessary, because there is nothing static and fixed in the world. This type of leadership demonstrates open-mindedness while tolerating ambiguity and volatility. As a leadership archetype, we call this *the Wise*.

As philosopher Theodore Zeldin writes: "Nothing influences our ability to cope with the difficulties of our existence so much as the context in which we view them; the more contexts we can choose between, the less do the difficulties appear to be inevitable and insurmountable".[4]

Context-awareness will help leaders to know the realities of their stakeholders, be they subordinates or suppliers and customers, and how they are all connected in the value chain. This corresponds to the six new beliefs that we explained in Chapter 3. If they fail to pay sufficient attention to this, they will fail as leaders in our journey to TVC. They will not be able to make the best decisions and they will not succeed in seeing these decisions through. This is exactly what is happening among leaders today: in spite of good intentions they oftentimes fail to connect with the actual reality of people today.

Researchers Metcalf and Benn explain this high degree of failure: "Leadership for sustainability requires leaders of extraordinary abilities. These are likely to be leaders who can read and predict through complexity, can think through complex problems, engage groups in dynamic adaptive organizational change and can manage emotion appropriately".[5]

Authors Navi Radjou and Prasad Kaipa, who have studied and consulted for nearly 100 CEOs who had to deal with large-scale crises, describe this as follows:

We need leaders who not only rely on their survival instincts or find opportunistic ways to leverage a crisis. We need leaders who consciously use their intuition, logic and emotions to choose appropriate business responses that also benefit society at large. We need wise leaders.[6]

In line with this quote, we would define wisdom as a well-configured synthesis of (affect-laden) intuition and reason. This of course requires context, but it also requires decision-making and judgment skills regarding the dilemma at hand. So while the Wise is rooted on understanding the context, wisdom is more than observing the context alone.

We saw this manifested in how Barack Obama handled the financial crisis at the start of his presidency. The crisis had given him an urgent platform for action on which he ran his campaign, yet the decisions he had to make were unprecedented in nature and scope. There was no textbook for solving a crisis that threatened to stall the entire global economy. Through a combination of context awareness, reasoning and intuition, the decisions that the new US president made calmed the US markets remarkably fast and well.[7]

Leadership reflection

We are confronted with a world full of paradoxes and contradictions every day. A message on social media, which may well be stripped of context, can cause an uproar and lead to millions of reaction which ask us – as leaders – to respond as well. So when we engage with some big debate or perceived outrage on these platforms, we should take the issues seriously, but also pause to ask ourselves: what's the context here? What really matters? What would be the response of "the Wise" at this moment?

Consciousness: The Learner

The faculty of consciousness refers to a fundamental human faculty, after which the *Homo sapiens* are called. The Sages of the past considered this the most important feature of a human being. The maxim "Know Thyself", attributed to Socrates, was inscribed in the Temple of Apollo in Delphi. In fact, modern biologists consider "cognition" to be the defining quality of life.[8]

We define it as the archetype of "the Learner", because it is exactly this quality of our mind that enables us to learn and adjust to a changing environment. And in a world of accelerating change, this is more important than ever. In the words of Arie de Geus, a former Shell top executive and business theorist, "The ability to learn faster than your competitors may be the only sustainable competitive advantage".

While the Wise is turned outwardly to the world and thus context awareness is characterized as outer awareness, the Learner represents *inner awareness,* aimed at growing one's own inner capacity and understanding. You could say that outer awareness and inner awareness complement each other.

Psychologist Carol Dweck has dedicated her career to understanding this learning aspect of the human being. She observed that there are roughly two mindsets that present a world of difference: fixed mindsets versus growth mindsets.[9] Fixed mindsets, as the term indicates, are static and occur when one tries to fit the world into one's set beliefs and ideas, and also see oneself as a fixed entity.

This fixed mindset provides a sense of short-term security, but in the longer run it will cause a lot of problems, as the reality tends to outgrow the scope of this mindset. Growth mindsets, however, provide flexibility and the opportunity to learn. It will see circumstances in life as an invitation to grow and develop. People with growth mindsets tend to be more successful and fulfilled in their lives and work.[10]

Therefore, a successful leader should have the capacity to reframe challenges and setbacks as learning opportunities. As the modern world is so rapidly changing and complexity is increasing, this could be the most fundamental quality for sustainability leadership.

Mahatma Gandhi said: "Live as if you were to die tomorrow. Learn as if you were to live forever". Marc Benioff, the CEO of Salesforce, expresses the same attitude: "I look at every failure as a learning experience and try to spend time with my failures. I stew on them for a while until I pick out some nugget from them that I can take forward".[11]

The Learner does not imply any "formal learning" or the intellect, and it is a quality of mind that is available to all humans, educated or not. Hamdi Ulukaya, Founder and CEO of Chobani, nicely illustrates this:

> I didn't have a business degree. I didn't have experience to work in somebody else's office. I never built or ran a department. So I was on this journey, and when the time came to make a decision, I was just going with my gut.

Leadership reflection

Take a moment to become aware of your own mind: close your eyes, take a few deep relaxed breaths and then notice your thoughts, feeling and sensations as they pass through your mind. Let go of any distractions in the outer world. What do you experience? What do you see that you may not have noticed if you had continued your outer work? Is there anything that you can stop doing or do differently? Self-awareness is a training that can greatly expand the scope of information that you pick up, leading to different decisions and actions.

Paul Ingram, who teaches leadership at Columbia University, concludes:

> I think the two qualities that are defining successful leaders at this moment are a capacity for ongoing learning and the ability to lead cultures. Learning, because business is evolving and organizations are only going to be more dynamic in the future. The executives who have been the most successful over time have been great learners. Then there's the capacity to lead cultures. Culture and strategy are the defining inputs, the differentiators, which determine whether organizations succeed or fail. They're both critically important, however strategy is easier to learn. And while leading the culture is learnable, it's also an art that takes practice. It's the rarer skill, and I think the best leaders of the next generation are going to be great learners who will be artful leaders of the culture.[12]

Connectedness: The Connector

We all know that successful leaders need to possess the ability to connect with various stakeholders and foster partnerships by engaging them wholeheartedly in the task at hand. With the holistic, end-to-end, long-term, impact-orientated, outside-in form of leadership that TVC calls for, the need for connected leadership and a concordant connected culture is even more pressing.

We call this leadership archetype "the Connector" who has the capacity to authentically connect to a wide range of people beyond one's own organization. The Connector is the quality that can build a culture. Said differently, leaders need to be equipped with advanced social and emotional skills to relate to and connect with multiple stakeholders, while managing social tensions, conflicts and dilemmas. This is also known as "emotional intelligence", defined by psychologist Daniel Goleman.[13] Most important here is to recognize the different needs, interests and views of others both close to the organization and further away. In contrast to the Wise, the Connector is an affective state of mind, apt in showing empathy, care and compassion.

Bill George, the former CEO of Medtronics, refers to this quality as follows: "I am not trying to diminish the role of the intellect. I am saying that we also have to lead with our hearts, because that's how we build connected relations. This means that we practice our values, we practice in the way we talk and behave".[14]

Dorothee D'Herde, Head of Sustainable Business, Vodafone Group, described this skill as "demonstrating collective vulnerability". Listening to all stakeholders with an open mind because "you can't have all the answers – and empathy can build bridges"[15]

Hamdi Ulukaya, Founder and CEO of Chobani, writes:

> Just about anyone can make a good product, but it's the people that count. In the end, it's the employees who will take it from a kitchen-table

idea to the next level. There are a lot of important things in business, but the people portion comes first.[16]

The Connecter can start small: connecting to another individual, your colleague, a client, a community that you are part of. This is essential in the TVC context, which extends the connection from the individual to the collective, from organization to society and from the shareholder/customer to the value network. There is no limit to connection – which we will explain below in more detail.

Centeredness: The Grounder

The Grounder is associated with our physical existence – our embodied experience and our sense of belonging to the earth; hence, in the context of sustainability there is a correlation to respecting and preserving our natural habitat (linked to New Belief 4: Planetary Health).

In leadership terms, the Grounder refers to "what we stand for", our roots, principles and values. This is about connection to roots and values, but also to this notion of balance over time, cycle after cycle. Circularity would require that cycles present a certain homeostasis around a core of certain values that one is closely connected to, making sure that these cycles, in the end, balance out and do not just escalate.[17]

The most enduring companies are continually adapting in a shifting environment, yet remain steadfast through values when everything is in motion. Like a bamboo tree, these companies stay deeply rooted in their core, which enables them to bend with the strongest wind without breaking.

Just after the outbreak of COVID-19, the Ford motor company made the surprising decision to make masks and ventilators. Ford's chairman Bill Ford Jr. explained this in words that echo the Grounder:

> We've been around 117 years. We were the arsenal of democracy during two World Wars, we built iron lungs for polio victims. Nobody's talked about the financial implications [of making masks and ventilators], because this is a national emergency. We'll sort all of that out later.[18]

The Grounder is linked to having a sense of purpose – knowing what drives you and why you do what you do. Over the past decade, "purpose" has become a management watchword. Most organizations have defined a mission statement, but this can only come to life when it is connected to the personal purpose of the leadership. Such purpose is personal, in the sense that it is unique for each person, but it is also directed toward something beyond oneself – sometimes called a "higher purpose". HBR author Nick Graig writes in *The Power of Purpose*: "Purpose is not a cause, a passion, an aspiration, or the sum of your values. Purpose is that unique gift that you bring to the world".[19] Importantly, in this definition, purpose is described in terms of your contribution to the outside world.

This is a leadership attitude that generates self-confidence and responsibility, as a ground state, regardless of external circumstances. Friedrich Kuhn, partner at executive search firm Egon Zehnder, describes this quality "being grounded in yourself", which he says can serve as the leader's anchor point in challenging times.[20] Leaders with a strong core mission tend to be patient and stable, even in the midst of chaos.

The root of the word courage is *cor*, the Latin word for heart. Centered in our hearts, courage rises. We can overcome what frightens us, face pain or grief, discover what endows our lives with meaning and purpose, and become a leader people trust.

Harvard Business School Professor, Nancy Koehn, defines a *courageous leader* as "an individual who's capable of making himself or herself better and stronger when the stakes are high and circumstances turn against that person".[21] She goes on to say, "Most of our lives, we're beset by crises. Courageous leaders are not cowed or intimidated. They realize that, in the midst of turbulence, there lies an extraordinary opportunity to grow and rise".

We often see the power of purpose manifested in great leaders. Mahatma Gandhi was a little known lawyer from South Africa with no formal power and with very few relationships in India, who purely on the basis of his own inner beliefs and convictions, with a heart for justice and equality, unleashed a successful political revolution in India. This is the quality of the Grounder.

We saw Paul Polman display this quality when he was CEO of Unilever. He describes purpose in the following words:

> You have to be driven by something. Leadership is not just about giving energy but it's unleashing other people's energy, which comes from buying into that sense of purpose. But if that purpose isn't strong enough in a company, if the top doesn't walk the talk, then the rest will not last long. The key thing for CEOs is to make that purpose a part of your operating model.[22]

Creativity: The Visionary

The Visionary stands for the archetypal leadership quality of developing a vision or a dream for the future, one that inspires others to follow in realizing this vision. John F. Kennedy spoke of "Putting a Man on the Moon" to rally people around America's race against communism in the Cold War. Martin Luther King drew on this Visionary power in his speech "I have a dream" to inspire a powerful movement for social change and justice. Their dreams inspired many others, up to this very day.

In a business context, think of Steve Jobs who realized ahead of many others how the transformational power of computers would change business and society. Steve Jobs' definition of leadership is telling: "Leadership is to do what you love to do, otherwise you will give up. Then dream big and develop a great daring vision. Surround yourself with great people and go beyond the fear of failure".[23]

An important aspect of this quality is to dream beyond what is possible today; it is a step into the unknown. Management scholar Jim Collins described this as the ability to set Wilde Hairy Audacious Goals.[24] "The best goals are the ones we have no clue how to get to", said Steve Howard – Chief Sustainability Officer, Temasek and Co-Chair of We Mean Business Coalition.[25] It is perhaps most poetically expressed by author Antoine De Saint Exupéry: "If you want to build a ship, don't gather people together to collect wood and don't assign them tasks and work, but rather teach them to long for the immensity of the sea".

At the same time, we are not speaking of some sort of faraway utopian ideal. The vision should project a clear unambiguous point on the horizon, which engages and stimulates others in participating in a process of co-creation and allows for collective leadership to emerge.

The collective dimension is important. It is not just a matter of a visionary CEO who rallies everyone around him, but a genuinely collectively felt perspective, which can only be generated when stakeholders are actively engaged in the creation of the vision. It is also important that vision and goals should be realistic and achievable, ensuring that sustainable ideas and strategies can be turned into action. In other words, the Visionary should not lose touch with where we stand today. Thus, the Visionary leader will set a point on the horizon with a realistic roadmap on how to get there, and he is also willing to use this for accountability and continuous learning with the collective. This is linked to the sixth new belief of long-term impact.

Competence: The Warrior

The Warrior is another primal archetype of leadership, which represents qualities such as competence, drive, energy, passion and persistence. In the Growth Triangle, we have seen this quality often in hierarchical and transactional terms. Here the leader has a formal position of *power over* other people, their subordinates or direct reports – basically all followers. One leads, the rest follows. The assumption is that the leader has superior information and on this basis takes calculated rational decisions. A leader listens, analyzes and decides. Subsequently, leaders make sure the decision is followed through.

The quality of the Warrior, however, goes beyond this classical management interpretation. In the modern reality of complex, diverse and virtual teams, with multiple and often loosely connected stakeholders, people are less inclined to follow "power-over" based leadership. Frederic Laloux describes this shifting dynamic in his influential book *Reinventing Organizations*.[26] Inspired by the principles of "self-organization" that's prevalent in living systems (see page 41), Laloux argues that the top-down style of leadership is outdated and no longer needed.

However, natural living systems don't shy away from asserting a sense of power when they are confronted with external threats and competition. Conflict, scarcity and even war are part of the natural world, and these conditions require leaders to focus their attention fully on neutralizing the impending threat. This capacity of focusing, in essence, is the quality of the Warrior. It can be regarded as responsible competitiveness. In business terms, it is the quality of summoning all one's unique competencies, resources and capabilities into creating a specific outcome that creates rather than destroys value.

This quality makes the leader cognizant of what to do and what not to do – he can make clear and courageous choices. In this respect, it relates to how Michael Porter defines the essence of making strategy: "it is about making choices, trade-offs and deliberately choosing to be different". It is this quality that established the firm's competitive advantage, says Porter.[27]

We recognize this archetype in many ancient cultures, where the Warrior style represents a concentrated, outward-oriented focus in an effort to defend one's territory and claiming one's stake. While this could be expressed in a "war-like" manner, we have learned from anthropology that we should not label tribal warriors as "aggressive" but as strongly motivated by collective survival. The modern version of the Warrior is one that recognizes the major sustainability challenges as the threat that endangers the survival of our collective human tribe and musters the courage to avert these dangers – the *Sustainability Warrior*. The energy of this archetype is summed up in the words of Rose Marcario, Former CEO of Patagonia: "Take risks, have courage, and let's make a better world together".

(With regard to the six new beliefs, the energy of the Warrior is related to "Markets are transactions/relationships", because it is at the marketplace where firms assert their competence and put themselves and their products to test. In a way, the market is the competitive playground for business. In the TVC view, companies are not truly sustainable if the market does not accept their products and services. Said differently, it is through the marketplace that TVC firms make a positive difference for the world.)

Integration into a dynamic model

As can be expected from a living systems viewpoint, the TVC leadership qualities are dynamically related to each other. For example, the Connector represents the capacity for the system to be open and adapt (connectivity/symbiosis), while the Warrior represents the capacity to focus and close (compete/efficiency). Thus, the Warrior – our capacity to focus on results to ensure efficiency – will need to be balanced by the Connector – our capability to build and maintain high-quality connections – and vice versa. With the right balance, these qualities will ensure that the system is resilient and vibrant. If the Warrior and the Connector are not balanced, the system will either become too active or even aggressive (low Connector/high Warrior), or too meek, slow and accommodating (high Connector/low Warrior).

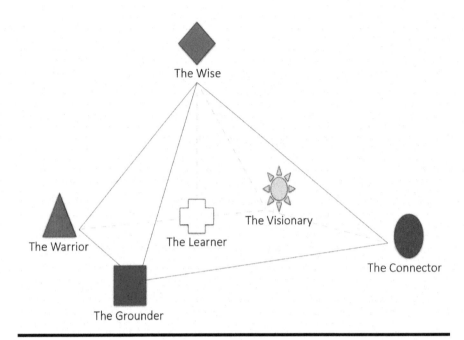

The Wise

The Visionary

The Warrior   The Learner

The Connector

The Grounder

Figure 8.1 The six leadership mindsets

Similarly, the Grounder ensures stability (homeostasis), while the Visionary facilitates renewal (regeneration), which can be somewhat contradictory. Thus, the qualities of the Grounder and the Visionary need to work together so that the system can evolve toward the desired future while retaining what's valuable from the past. If these forces are not balanced, the Grounder will cause complacency and rigidity (high Grounder/low Visionary) and the Visionary becomes too mobile and scattered (low Grounder/high Visionary).

In essence, the Learner and the Wise function as a process of cognition that allows the organism to learn and adjust to the changing context. The interplay between the Learner and the Wise represents to the full blossoming of our internal and external awareness, maintaining the dynamic balance between all other qualities, while each playing their role in the regeneration of the organism.

In this context, it is fitting to present the sixfold TVC mindset in a three-dimensional sphere in which the Learner and the Wise represent the central vertical axis and the other four archetypes four horizontal directions.

What is the relationship of this model with business sustainability? On the one hand, these six leadership qualities are linked to all living systems – be it ecosystems, people, or companies. On the other hand, sustainability is a sound equilibrium that all living systems (including humanity) should gravitate toward in order to stay healthy, which they will do as long as they dynamically balance all these six qualities.

It can be argued that the current system is unbalanced and unsustainable as the Growth Triangle fails to respect the larger ecological context (low Wise), is disconnected from vital stakeholders (low Connector) and is only motivated by activity with short-term financial results (high Warrior/low Visionary)

This will be taken further in Chapter 9.

Organization & Leadership: Eileen Fisher

Eileen Fisher, founded by her namesake in 1984, has been recognized as one of the top 500 women-owned businesses and one of the 25 best companies to work for. As of today, the fashion industry remains one of the most wasteful industries in the world as a result of many brands' tendencies to dispose of old garments and fabrics in landfills. Textiles are purchased from countries with poor labor standards and its production process consumes lots of water, energy and chemicals. Nonetheless, Eileen Fisher decided to adopt environmentally conscious manufacturing practices years before it became a trendy cause. In 2009 the brand decided to reduce the brand's reusable textiles waste, which has been a major issue many fashion brands have just now begun to address.

"Our environmental vision is holistic", says Shona Quinn, Director of Social Consciousness. "We believe in paying attention to what happens in the field, the dye house and our customers' washing machines. Our goal is to design out negative impacts – and design in positive change". These statements are obvious reflections of both *the Wise* (holistic vision) and *the Learner* (design in positive ways).

This Learner is also evident in the practice of starting all meetings with a minute of silence. Eileen Fisher explains:

> Mindfulness means slowing down enough to be thoughtful about what you're doing. It helps you see the need to get other viewpoints in order to see the whole. It brings more self-awareness –of how you feel, how you speak, how you treat others. Over time, it starts to weave itself into everything you do.[28]

In 2015 the company launched a bold plan toward the goal of 100% sustainability, which is an expression of the *Visionary*. "We don't want sustainability to be our edge, we want it to be universal", said Eileen Fisher. The firm reframed its mission from selling clothes toward serving and empowering women, who are the company's main customers and employees: "Use business as a force for change by making clothes that empower women and are responsibly designed from field to factory to closet".[29] This mission represents the *Grounder*.

The brand obviously also has a strong *Connector* quality, evident from the various Eileen Fisher initiatives to empower women, including through the communities in the supply chain. "I believe that a powerful collective energy emerges when women connect with other women", said Eileen Fisher. Finally, the *Warrior* is evident by Eileen's relentless focus on the essentials. Instead of going public, Eileen Fisher transferred shares to her employees and registered as a public benefit corporation (B-Corp).

These qualities steered the company into the direction of Triple Value: higher workforce motivation, higher brand profile and customer loyalty, and higher financial returns. By focusing on the needs of society (empowerment and well-being of women, clean production and worker conditions), the needs of clients (offering great design products to clients) and its own needs of staff well-being and better reputation, Eileen's Fisher is an example of the TVC approach. They evidently found strategic alignment among the needs of their stakeholders.

Light and shadow

Even though all these qualities are available in our mind, we do have a strong preference for some of them while others remain hidden and underutilized. You can say some are in the light while others are in the dark. We are habituated to a particular pattern of some archetypes which made us successful in the past, starting in childhood.

In many cases, we have found that leaders have a surplus of two or three of the six qualities, but they may be deficient in some of the others. Typically, people with strong Warrior quality may have a weaker Connector, and vice versa. The same applies to the contrasting qualities of Grounder and Visionary, which are oriented to the present and future, respectively.

When leaders rely too much on one quality, they may ignore other necessary competencies and lose balance as a consequence. The leader may have good intentions, but the lack of balance between the different qualities may cause his/her leadership to become ineffective. These patterns could lead to certain "performance gaps", causing the leader to underperform or even fail in critical competence areas.[30]

Moreover, when we are under stress, all these archetypes can turn into "their shadows", as Carl Jung called it. This can be triggered by particular conditions, like a critical incident or prolonged emotional tension and negligence in childhood. Some archetypes become suppressed while others become overcompensated.

People tend to default to patterns of the leadership archetype that we are most habituated to. The leader with the archetypical Warrior style will turn into a bulldozer when he feels challenged by unnecessary obstacles, yet it may be this impatient response that will alienate stakeholders that he will need further down the road in the sustainability transition. So a leader of this nature will need to cultivate the

Connector energy to make sure that he continues to see the perspective of others in the change process.

Conversely, the Connector can turn into the Pleaser – unable to draw boundaries and make decisions, aiming to generate consensus while action is required; the Grounder can become the Blocker – reluctant to be flexible and remain rigid and fixated on the current status quo, while change is inevitable and needed; and the Visionary can transform into the Dreamer – unable to accept the current reality and escaping into new ideas and plans, while neglecting the needs of the current business.

This is quite common among leaders who are leading toward sustainability. The CEO of French diary giant Danone, Emmanuel Faber, was a strong and vocal advocate of sustainability, yet he became a victim of two activist shareholders (who held but 3% of the shares) who blamed Faber for an underperforming stock price relative to competitors such as Nestlé and Unilever.[31] This happens when visionary qualities are not counterweighed by the qualities of the Warrior and the Grounder: research by Harvard indicated that CEOs who invest in sustainability but don't show commensurate financial growth run a high risk of being ousted.[32]

Obviously, the shadow archetypes undermine the leader's effectiveness and are major pitfalls on the path toward sustainability leadership. Therefore, we need to understand how to learn to cultivate all archetypes, recognizing their individual strengths as well as their collective power when all qualities are well-balanced and work in harmony. To achieve sustainability, in particular, requires all qualities to be strong and mutually supportive for the Sustainability Warrior to be effective.

Notes

1 Jung, C. G. (August 1, 1971). *"Psychological Types"*. Collected Works of C.G. Jung, Volume 6. Princeton, NJ: Princeton University Press.
2 Hull, R. F. C, ed. (2014). "Archetypes of the Collective Unconscious", *Collected Works of C.G. Jung, Volume 9 (Part 1): Archetypes and the Collective Unconscious*, Princeton, NJ: Princeton University Press, pp. 3–41.
3 Campbell, J. (1986). *The Hero with a Thousand Faces*. Princeton: Princeton University Press.
4 Zeldin, T. (1994). *An Intimate History of Humanity*. New York: HarperCollins.
5 Metcalf, L., & Benn, S. (2013). Leaders for sustainability: An evolution of leadership ability. *Journal of Business Ethics, 112*(3), 369–384.
6 Radjou, N., & Kaipa, P. (2013). From Smart to Wise: Acting and Leading With Wisdom. (Jossey-Bass, 2013). Sloan Management Review – April 2020: https://sloanreview.mit.edu/article/leading-with-your-head-and-your-heart/.
7 Obama, B. (2020). *A Promised Land* (1 ed.). New York: Crown Publishing Group.
8 Capra, F. "The Santiago Theory of Life and Cognition." la revista Be-Vision 9.1 (1986): 59–60; Maturana, H. R., & Varela, F. J. (1980). *Autopoiesis and Cognition. The Realization of the Living*. Dordrecht: Reidel, p. 13.
9 Dweck, C. S. (2006). *Mindset: How you can fulfill your potential*. London: Robinson.
10 Ibid.

11 http://meaningring.com/2019/09/07/life-advice-from-marc-benioff/.

12 April 16, 2019. www.europeanbusinessreview.com/empowering-your-leadership-at-the-pulse-of-business-in-new-york-city/.

13 Goleman, D. (1996). *Emotional Intelligence. Why It Can Matter more than IQ.* London: Bloomsbury.

14 Quoted in Tideman, S. G. (2016). *Business as an Instrument of Societal Change – In Conversation with H.H. the Dalai Lama.* Sheffield, UK: Greenleaf Publishing.

15 Quoted in Korn Ferry report, The Rise of the Chief Sustainability Officer. February 24, 2021.

16 Strom, S. (April 16, 2016). *Now at Chobani, it is not just the yoghurt that's rich. New York Times.* www.nytimes.com/2016/04/27/business/a-windfall-for-chobani-employees-stakes-in-the-company.html.

17 The idea of a linear experience of time and a linear narrative of history seems related to Christianity (see, e.g., White LT, Jr. 1967. The historical roots of our ecologic crisis. *Science, 155,* 1203–1207).

18 Radjou, N., & Kaipa, P. (April 24, 2020). Leading-with-your-head-and-your-heart. Retrieved from: https://sloanreview.mit.edu/article/.

19 Craig, N. (2018). *Leading from Purpose: Clarity and the Confidence to Act When It Matters Most.* New York: Hachette Books.

20 Interview with Friedrich Kuhn.

21 Koehn, N. F. (2017). *Forged in Crisis: The Power of Courageous Leadership in Turbulent Times.* New York: Scribner.

22 www.theguardian.com/sustainable-business/unilever-ceo-paul-polman-purpose-profits.

23 www.businessinsider.com/steve-jobs-quality-sets-apart-great-leaders-2019-4?international=true&r=US&IR=T.

24 Collins, J. (2001). *Good to Great – Why Some Companies Make the Leap, and Some Others Don't.* New York: Harper Business.

25 Korn Ferry report (2020). How sustainability leadership can unlock business resilience, innovation and future performance. Retrieved from: https://infokf.kornferry.com/the-rise-of-the-CSO.htm.

26 Laloux, F. (2014). *Reinventing Organizations: A Guide to Creating Organizations Inspired by the Next Stage of Human Consciousness.* Brussels: Nelson Parker.

27 Porter, M. E. (1985) *The Competitive Advantage: Creating and Sustaining Superior Performance.* New York: Free Press.

28 www.eileenfisher.com/ns/images/ourcompany/inthemedia/pdf/2014/ns_mindful_us_dec2013_inside.pdf.

29 https://cfda.com/news/how-eileen-fisher-is-the-ultimate-sustainable-label; www.thegeniusworks.com/2018/10/sustainable-fashion-eileen-fisher-has-become-a-leader-in-clothing-with-a-conscience/.

30 Fox E. (2013). *Winning from Within.* New York: Harper Collins.

31 www.reuters.com/article/us-danone-management-idUSKBN2B60PN (Retrieved March 14, 2021)

32 Hubbard, T., Christensen, D., & Graffin, S. (2017). *Higher Highs and Lower Lows: The Role of Corporate Social Responsibility in CEO Dismissals. Strategic Management Journal, 38*(11), 2255–2265.

Chapter 9

Dealing with complexity

The systems mindset in action

In this chapter we will look at how we can cultivate the systems mindset, an essential leadership quality, which is necessary for addressing the unprecedented and complex sustainability challenge. We will start by looking at the narrow efficiency mindset and related values that characterize the Growth Triangle, before moving to exploring how leaders can influence complex systems "from within" by accessing "social fields".

This brings us to the need of marrying the qualities of the Wise and the Learner (the Open Mind), with the power of the Connector that represents motivation and compassion (Open Heart), in order to embrace the full systems perspective.

Next, we will explore the concept of "Triple Purpose" which will ensure the overall direction as well as the ethical dimension of leadership, to arrive at a description of the "Sustainability Warrior", whose role it is to execute on TVC systems leadership.

We will bring this together in a comprehensive TVC leadership model with a systems perspective on value creation, which shows the way toward the zenith of sustainability leadership.

Overcoming the narrow efficiency mindset: Expanding the mind and heart

Along the principles of the Growth Triangle, most companies have been built as efficient machines for delivering value for shareholders. With it came a wide array of management tools for rigorously analytical and quantified decision-making and driving efficiency. This has installed an "efficiency mindset" in modern business leadership. Many leaders believe that this is their main task – driving results in the most efficient manner.

As said, the Growth Triangle and Cycle of Sustainability represent different and often contrasting sets of values – with an invisible glass ceiling in between. Here is a sample of what these different value sets would look like:

Growth Triangle (efficiency mindset)	Circle of Sustainability (systems mindset)
Transactional	Relational
Centrality	Diversity
Control	Trust
Dependability	Creativity
Quantity	Quality
Precision	Experimentation
Stable	Agile
Accountability	Transparency

Each of the two columns represents a particular worldview.

As we have seen in Chapter 8, the left column is the manifestation of the "narrow" Warrior, operating without awareness of a larger and changing context that the leader is operating in. In the left column worldview, the qualities of the Wise, the Learner and the Connector are underdeveloped and underrepresented.

That is, companies are low in context awareness, have a limited understanding of their role in the value chain and have a limited connectedness with their stakeholders. They typically function as "rational agents" and preset production machines, with little sensitivity to the wider societal and ecological context they operate in.

As a by-effect, the company's strategy is aimed at short-term financial and singular value creation.

Without the awareness of the Wise, the narrow efficiency mindset fails to see what business needs to do in order to achieve sustainability goals such as recyclability, zero waste, cradle-to-cradle, circular economy and ecological footprint. These objectives require an open mind, a co-creative attitude and a willingness to engage with multiple external stakeholders, empower employees, open up to new ideas, and turn them into innovative products and services – these are all qualities engrained in the right-hand column worldview.

With these qualities, leaders will be capable of creating value in *a systemic way* within the stakeholder value network. This systems view will infuse the Warrior with a new direction turning it into the "Sustainability Warrior". Instead of pursuing narrow efficiency goals, the Warrior will now drive sustainable value creation.

Nonetheless, transitioning to the right column is often hard to do. Managers with values of the left column often think of innovators with values on the right as frivolous and impractical. The tension might be described and experienced in many different ways. For example, as *realistic* versus *dreaming,* or *rigor* versus *intuition. Hard* versus *soft.*

These dichotomies are misleading: we have no choice but to recognize both values sets and evolve from a partial to a holistic understanding of value creation – and of ourselves, for that matter.

Ilham Kadri, CEO and Chair of the Executive Committee of Solvay, brings this home in the following words: "We need to unlearn what we have done in the past and think of building up new competencies for future leaders around sustainability and circularity towards reinventing new forms of progress".[1]

Activating the Wise – the systems mindset

How do we arrive at this systems mindset? First, we will need to cultivate the Wise, whose quality is the ability to think holistically by considering actions at multiple levels of complexity. This has become the most important leadership quality, simply because today's challenges reveal a nature of systemic interconnectedness. We need a systems mindset to deal with a systems crisis.

To be precise, the new Triple Value perspective requires the leader to recognize that the environment of the organizations is actually much larger than normally conceived. Traditionally, companies see their immediate environment as markets and customers. Now they have to see the societal and ecological domain as well.

It is true that this perspective will enhance the complexity of business. Yet it is possible to find a way to "cut through" this complexity by recognizing the dynamic of the *value chain* – the cycle of cause and effect set in motion by companies, extending beyond the market into society and nature. This in effect represents the *outside-in perspective* distinguishes TVC from earlier iterations of CSR.

The value chain (or better: the value system) is not just a concept: it reflects the actual way that value is co-created by stakeholders, through a chain of real causes and effects, centered about *the needs* of each stakeholder. For business to move toward Triple Value creation, they will have to identify the respective needs of the stakeholders in the value chain and find ways to collectively serve these needs.

The needs perspective is essential for understanding living systems in general and TVC in particular. To really understand and act upon the needs, we will need to invoke the Learner and Connector.

Leadership reflection: Value system

Reflect on the core product or service that your company is making. What people and factors go into making the product? Look at all causes and conditions that have gone into its production, however small and insignificant. Draw these on a piece of paper. Then look at what happens after you have sold the product. Whose needs are you serving? Who benefits? What will happen with the people who benefit – what causal chain will your customer's experience set in motion? What happens with the waste or residue of the product? What residual needs are you *not* serving or compromising? Make this "value system" as long as possible in time and space.

While *the Wise* determines the *scope* of the leadership, we will also need to know how leaders, as they develop their minds, expand their capacity of systems leadership. This brings us to *the Learner*, the quality of *curiosity* and ability to cultivate new mindsets and insights, as well as *the Connector*, which represent the *motivation* of the leadership, directed at genuinely serving the *needs* of the value network.

Once we have evoked these three qualities, we will turn to the remaining three archetypes of the Grounder, the Visionary and the Warrior. We will conclude with an integrated model for Triple Value creation based on the six archetypes.

Dealing with complexity – awakening our awareness

First, let's remind ourselves of why the Learner and the Wise, being qualities of awareness, are ideally suited to handle complexity. A complex "living" system, such as global warming, pandemics or the food supply chain, cannot be known and understood in the same way as a linear nonliving material system, such as a car or

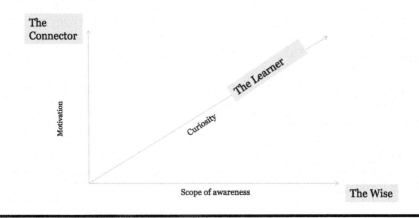

Figure 9.1 Activating the Learner

computer. The main distinction is this: in a complex system our own action (or nonaction) influences the behavior of the system.

Complex systems scientist Melanie Mitchell defines complex systems as "a system in which large networks of components with no central control and simple rules of operation give rise to complex collective behavior, sophisticated information processing, and adaptation via learning or evolution".[2]

Since complex systems are open systems, they use and produce information from both their internal and external environments, or – we could say – they are a mind of their own. The moment that we become aware of the system, we can interact with the information processed in the system. For example, the way you talk about your company actually shapes the reality of your business. There is no company "out there" existing independent from how you and your coworkers perceive and describe it.

Thus, through our faculty of awareness – represented by the Learner and the Wise – we can communicate with the system. This is because, as Mitchell asserts, our brains are themselves complex systems, where we store, access, represent and generate information. Learning and understanding occur through a dynamic and non-linear process of pattern matching between internal neuronal activity and external input. Our minds absorb and generate information at the same time – information is literally a process of forming the mind. Said in another way: the outer "objective" system and our inner "subjective" perception of it are not separate.

In an attempt to understand how complex systems can be "managed", social scientists have sought to mirror the insights from complexity science. This work was pioneered by Kurt Lewin, who conceived of the *social field*, defined as "a dynamic field that interacts with human consciousness, which are conceived of as mutually interdependent".[3] In this conception, there is no individual that can exist apart from a social field – a context created by interacting humans in multiple dimensions, as individuals, organizations and societies.

MIT scholar Otto Scharmer built on the work of Lewin when he formulated the "Theory U" as means to lead complex adaptive systems.[4] He points out that there is a difference between social systems and social fields. Whereas a social system is perceived from the "outside", the concept of social field is used to describe a social system from an "inside perspective"; how it *feels like* to be operating within such a system. Similarly, Scharmer speaks of "eco-system awareness", which describes "the inside" of our relationship with the ecosystems and sustainability.[5]

Leadership reflection: Practice "Meta-awareness"[6]

This is a meditation practice without focusing on a particular object, incorporating the totality of experience. It requires a "zooming out" to a perspective in which you can observe yourself *and* your context. In this practice, we make no distinction between inner or outer, but allow all phenomena to arise, observing outer and inner sensations, without conceptualization, judgment or interpretation. The mind is open, present and nonjudgmental, while it is fully aware of all experiences and sensations in and around you.

When you train your mind in this way, you will cultivate "meta-awareness" which strengthens your capacity for systems leadership; you will be able to direct your awareness to any complex challenge, without prematurely compartmentalizing or judging it or giving in to emotions of impatience and overwhelm. You can penetrate any social field while retaining your open mind. You will learn to truly be "with the system" and influence it in the process.

In the terminology of TVC leadership, it is the quality of the Learner that makes us aware of the inner field that makes up the system.

The power of the Learner

We will encounter the resistance to change, both inside and around us. When we progress along the leadership path toward handling more complexity and taking larger responsibilities, we will encounter barriers and platforms, which seem to halt our progress. We will encounter doubt, fear and cynicism. Why me? Why is not everyone doing it – or why are people resisting it? Is it possible at all?

What to do about this? For success it is essential to activate the Learner, which quite literally can "enlighten" hidden or repressed aspects of our consciousness, our organization and our context.

That's why we need to consider that the most important leadership tool is first and foremost the leader's own mind: it is important that the leader learns to take care of herself. Such self-care is not selfishness or narcissism, but a self-management practice which ensures that we don't deplete our batteries and renew ourselves as we overcome our inner and outer foes. Mindfulness practice can be a great gateway toward activating our Learner.

The quality of the Learner gives us the opportunity to be self-aware, to understand our emotions and learn not to take them at face value. We can observe and accept our emotions and discover the freedom to change them.

This is well described by Victor Frankl who survived Nazi prison camps by discovering the power of his mind. In spite of being stripped of all physical freedoms, he found inner freedom from the way he chose to see himself and the world. In his book *Man's Search for Meaning*, Frankl writes: "Everything can be taken from a man but one thing: the last of the human freedoms – to choose one's attitude in any given set of circumstances, to choose one's own way"[7]

Cultivating this type of leadership entails a form of learning that goes beyond the intellect, but touches on our deepest beliefs and mindset.

This seems a tall order. The good news is that we have been doing this from early age – this is the way we learned to grow into mature adults. Why not continue learning and growing? We may consider ourselves to be a mature adult, but in the face of the unprecedented challenges we are still in kindergarten. We need to revive our innate curiosity and rekindle the playful growth mindset that most of us experienced, at least at certain moments in our childhood.

Science: Vertical development

The field of adult development psychology provides an interesting perspective on the Learner.

This field goes back to child psychologist Jean Piaget who studied how children learn. He observed that children are learning by adapting progressively complex schemes or progressive stages.[8] Each stage of learning includes and then transcends the earlier stages. When children grow up, they move from a dependent stage (young child) to stages of independence (adolescent), and finally to interdependency (mature adult). At the level of interdependency, the child is no longer inclined to stick to simple strategies such as attachment to its parent (*dependent*) or rebellion against them (*independent*). Rather, the child can handle a degree of complexity and can make a more autonomous decision. As he continues to evolve in life, he can grow in his understanding of the *interdependent* nature of the world, as well as the capacity of taking responsibility for the world.[9]

While this is a regular maturity process, we can apply these insights onto the field of leadership development, as the learning of leaders evolves along a similar stage-by-stage trajectory toward handling increasing complexity. Scholars tend to make a distinction between *horizontal development* – which is about adding more knowledge and skills – and *vertical development* – which entails the expansion of what an individual can pay attention to, and, therefore, what he or she can influence.[10] With vertical learning, the leader's wisdom is growing. We can also say that the *capacity of leadership* has increased.

Leaders who have developed "vertically" and gained the interdependent mindset can live more comfortably into paradox and are able to hold polarities; they can be with multiple perspectives and see connections and systems more easily. Once people see that their identity is multilayered, paradox becomes easier to accept. There is less personal involvement and judgment with what is observed in a way, and a greater ability to be with everything as it is.

Obviously, the interdependent mindset is an essential precondition for leaders to take on a systems perspective required for TVC at multiple levels of complexity and interdependency.

Now that we have awakened the Wise and the Learner, it does not stop here: we are coactive participants in the system, impacting the resilience of the system. The question is: how do we make it more resilient? This turns us to the Connector, which represents our motivation. Do we interact with fear or compassion, with anxiety or confidence?

This is especially for TVC: nowadays every leader says that he cares about stakeholders, but in many cases it is just window dressing. So how to do this genuinely? How to distinguish authentic sustainable value creation from inauthentic greenwashing?

The motivation to care: The Connector

As a Connector, it is not enough to only see the needs of the stakeholders, but we should also try to *feel* them empathically. Do you *really care* about all the stakeholders in the value chain? Will you allow that care to grow into a sense of responsibility not just for your own kin and tribe, but for the whole value chain, including society and nature? And will your motivation be strong enough so as to move you to action?

In fact, TVC leadership develops along three dimensions. One is the leader's capacity of awareness, which enables him to recognize the various levels of complexity – the "open mind". The other is the leader's motivation that is the wish to care for and serve others – the "open heart". In between these dimensions, the Learner is manifested opening up to and welcoming the world, with a willingness to go beyond fears and conventions that hold us back.

We can depict this in Figure 9.2. One axis represents the leader's awareness of complexity, the Wise, while the other is his motivation to take care and feel compassion for increasing levels of stakeholders, or the Connector.

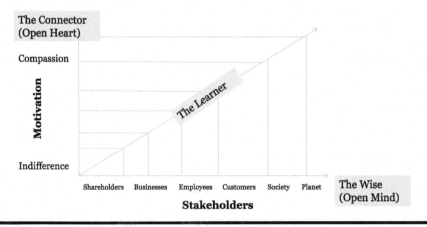

Figure 9.2 The Learner – Open Heart and Mind

Systems compassion

At the highest level of connectedness, the leader is motivated by compassion – the willingness to serve the needs of others and act on it. This needs to be practiced in stages. You can't simply leap into these higher states of motivation without training and preparation.

Thus, compassion starts with care for those who are close to you, specifically one's direct reports, one's team and one's support staff. The next stage is to care for all employees and shareholders. This will be the ingredient for building an authentic culture in the firm. Next, leaders will need to learn to extend their care to the needs of their customers primarily because their business' success depends on how well they serve them. This should be more than caring for "market share", but a genuine understanding and appreciation of the customer's experience, by relating to them as human beings with authentic needs.

In the context of TVC, leaders will need to extend their care even further: they need to open their heart for society as a whole and the ecosystem that makes life possible. With regard to society, they should think of the services provided by schools and hospitals, as well as the democratic process, the judicial system and the cultural sector. Then, the circle of care can be extended to natural parks, clean air, drinkable water, animal welfare, biodiversity, regenerative soil, chemical-free food – the list is long.

Importantly, compassion is not just empathy, but a willingness to explore the real needs of others, leading to action.[11] Compassion is the next developmental step after empathy. The more you feel the needs of others, the more likely you will be moved to act. In this sense, compassion transcends and includes empathy.[12]

When Open Mind and Open Heart are practiced in parallel, the leader will evolve along progressive stages in TVC leadership capacity. When leaders become fully present to those around them, they are better able to manage situations simply because they more clearly see what is really going on. They can learn to effectively respond to the world around them, even in times of adversity, with less negativity, anxiety or aggression, and more kindness, courage, and creativity.[13]

System: Unlocking the power of the crowd

A potent symbol of the Connector was the climate march by school children in the spring of 2019, taking place in many European countries. The Swedish school kid Greta Thunberg, then 16 years of age, who did not have any formal role, asked the children in the world to follow her in a strike demanding climate action from the world powers. By simply speaking her heart – using her own informal power – she was followed by millions of children and received global attention. A few months later, she was elected as Time Magazine's "Leader of the Year" and nominated for countless rewards (which she refused to accept). "You say you love your children above all else, and yet you are stealing their future in front of their eyes", Greta said.

There is enormous power in the relationships that we have, our trusted family, friend and colleagues, on which we can count in many circumstances. These relations can give us vital support, information, advice and access to others. The better the quality and quantity of our relationships, the more power we can derive from them. This is the quality of the Connector. When groups of people decide to move as a collective, it is very difficult for others to resist it. We saw it when the Berlin wall collapsed and East Block regimes, one after the other, crumbled under public pressure. With the power of social media (and – obviously – guidance by wise leaders), the quality of connectedness can easily turn loose individuals into cohesive tribes.

The quality of connectedness will help leaders in building coalitions and partnerships to address collective issues that we cannot solve alone. Many challenges today are systemic in nature that can only be met by collective systemic response. This is a quality that TVC leaders will need to master; they will need to learn systems-leadership skills that engage others in cocreating their future.

Leadership reflection

Start with your own team: awaken the power of the crowd even if it is a small group of direct reports. Engage them in a co-creative field, exploring their connectedness and visionary capacity. Ask them what they care about, what they believe in, what hopes they have for a better world? If done authentically, you will be amazed how much energy a small team can generate.

Adaptation and emergence: The role of the Grounder and the Visionary

As we discussed in Part 1, complex systems have no central control – they are self-organizing. It is the collective actions of vast numbers of mutually interdependent actors that give rise to the complex, nonlinear and emergent patterns of behavior, aimed at adaptation and regeneration. Yet there is an important role for leadership to play, exactly because the system is open and interdependent: leaders are the nodes within the field and as such they have tremendous systems impact.

In fact, by becoming aware of the social field, leaders can become part of the process of "emergence" of the social system. Social fields can be qualified as generative or degenerative, which can be translated as healthy or not healthy, or resilient and not resilient.

Science: generative social fields

System scholars Peter Senge and Mette Boell have defined generative social fields in the following way. They possess the following characteristics:

- when phenomena consistently and intentionally arise within the field that are beneficial within a larger context – that is, contribute to well-being of a larger system
- when learning and collective creativity– realizing new outcomes and building new capacities – naturally and continuously takes place
- when well-being for those who co-generate the field is nurtured and grown naturally[14]

These findings are very relevant for leadership: we have the ability to help complex systems to increase toward collective well-being of its constituent parts. This is where the qualities of *the Grounder* and *the Visionary* come in; they enable the system to find purpose and meaning, which are causing the system to be generative rather than degenerative and evolve to a higher order of sustainability. By impacting collective well-being, the Visionary and the Grounder constitute the ethical compass of business leadership.

The time dimension: Daring to dream

Now that the scope of leadership has been expanded in space (i.e. more stakeholders), we should also expand it in terms of time. In particular, the needs of future generations, who will be the ultimate beneficiaries of sustainable development, are worthy of our care. The Native American Chief Seattle is quoted as saying: "We do not inherit the earth from our ancestors; we borrow it from our children".

In his book *The Good Ancestor*, contemporary philosopher Roman Krznaric writes:

> We live in the age of the tyranny of the now, driven by 24/7 news, the latest tweet, and the buy-now button. With such frenetic short-termism at the root of contemporary crises – from the threats of climate change to the lack of planning for a global pandemic – the call for long-term thinking grows every day.[15]

Krznaric suggests that if we want to be good ancestors and be remembered well by the next generations, we need to urgently recover and enrich our imaginative skills.

Indeed, he refers to the qualities of *Visionary*, who represents the time dimension in the TVC leadership model. Encouraged by the broadened context revealed by the Wise and the Connector, the Visionary is called in to "have a dream" of what the future could look like. The Visionary – in a process engaging major stakeholders – will set collective goals to create long-term sustainable value and inspire innovation to achieve these goals, so that the system can renew and regenerate itself.

The promise of Triple Purpose

We have seen that *the Grounder* represents one's ability to recognize one's purpose: the "why" of one's leadership expressed in the leader's unique contribution or gift to the world. Such purpose can "empower" the leader – it can be a source of inspiration, courage and determination. Jodi Berg, CEO of Vitamix, explains: "When you discover the commonality between your own purpose and that of your business, you can unleash your 'superpower'".

Leadership example: Jodi Berg, CEO of Vita Mix – the power of purpose

Jodi Berg, PhD, is the first woman CEO of Vitamix, a family-owned mid-market manufacturer of blending equipment for the consumer and food service markets.

Forbes Magazine recounts that it was a near-death experience at age 30 that gave Jodi's life a new perspective on life.[16] This second chance offered her a chance to develop a mindset of focusing on making a difference and providing people tools to thrive. Aside from her job as CEO, Jodi decided to pursue a PhD degree. She was especially intrigued by the question: "why are people who are driven by a higher 'purpose' distinct from people who are driven by 'goals'?" She also wanted to understand how the purpose of an organization and an employee's personal purpose have an effect on work performance.

As a researcher, Jodi determined that the societal purpose of companies had no significant impact on the employees' satisfaction with life, until it was connected to their personal purpose. A personal purpose –which provides meaning to their life – turns out to give people be more engaged and committed to their work, while also boosting their life satisfaction. Importantly, Jodi discovered that "companies can increase engagement and commitment by not only creating and sharing a company higher purpose but by helping employees identify their personal purpose".

As CEO, Jodi Berg took measures that made a purpose to become integral to the day-to-day operations at Vitamix. Jodi takes the time to talk with employees about personal purpose and has trained others to help new staff what they do really well and what gives them passion and energy. She calls this the "superpower". Jodi Berg is committed to creating a culture where every person knows their purpose and is encouraged to express it in a way that matters to them.

For the leader to be authentic and credible, such purpose should be shared between the leader and the company. In the context of TVC, as the leader has more awareness of who constitutes the company's value chain, he has more options to determine who should be the recipient of his unique gift. This will enable him to direct his shared purpose to serving the wider needs of society – the system as a whole. This is a crucial insight underpinning the TVC approach.

We define such a purpose as *Triple Purpose*, which arises when a personal purpose has grown into a purpose for the larger context in which the leader's organization operates. This was implicit in the words of Paul Polman describing his purpose in leading Unilever: "How can I help my company to serve society?"[17]

If done well, activating the Triple Purpose between people, business and society can become an avenue for a new level of organization performance – not just superpower, as Jody Berg calls it, but "sustainability superpower".

This process starts by clarifying the mission or purpose of the organization. Signe Spencer, a client research partner at the Korn Ferry Institute, who has studied purpose among his executive clients, states: "Without a stated purpose, leadership can be accused of 'purpose washing', which happens as companies' own actions don't reflect their publicly stated purpose". He continues:

Companies may declare to the world that maximizing profits isn't the end-all, be-all, but if they'll continue to act as if shareholder value is the only value to the corporation, they run a major reputation risk. Sooner or later, people begin to see you as a hypocrite and that, too, destroys value.[18]

Said differently, when companies commit to a societal purpose, their leaders will need to activate their own societal motivation and manifest this in tangible action. That's why the Grounder needs to work together with Visionary, as well as with Warrior (which we will discuss below) – this leads to a sound authentic purpose.

As Olivier Blum, Chief Strategy and Sustainability Officer, Schneider Electric, explains:[19] "Sustainability needs to be integral to your strategy, your business model, your value proposition and your culture".

Leadership example: Bill George and Medtronics

Bill George took a purpose-based approach to business with considerable success. In a coffee shop overlooking Lake Geneva, he told me how he had embedded a "shared purpose" at Medtronics, a multinational firm in medical devices such as pacemakers. Under Bill George's leadership, the firm went from three million people per year to ten million people per year.

After his wife was diagnosed with cancer, he decided to put the care for his wife and family above his career. He started a daily meditation practice that he has kept up over the decades.[20] He reformulated the company's purpose from increasing revenue and earnings per share into causing people to restore to full and active life and health by producing superior medical devices. This is a "shared purpose" between the beneficiaries of their products and the workers and shareholders of Medronics. In our mind, this is a Triple Purpose because the interests of the workers, the company and societal benefits are aligned. The key to success, Bill told us, was to always convey this Triple Purpose to people in the company because that's what inspires them, not the stock price or the earnings. When the company's mission inspires people, they will produce better quality work, which in turn will drive customer satisfaction and financial results.

In summary: the discovery of Triple Purpose is the sweet spot of TVC leadership. It is the natural outcome of activating the Wise, the Learner and the Connector – firmly expanding the scope of leadership into serving society – and linking them to the Visionary and the Grounder, which determine the benefits for stakeholders.

If done well, this will unleash a force that enables a company to take on the grand challenges of today and reframe them into opportunities for internal growth and learning, leading to enhanced business performance as well. This illustrates that in the TVC context, purpose, ethics and sustainable performance go hand in hand.

The Sustainability Warrior

Now that the Wise, Learner, Connector, Visionary and Grounder are activated and empowered, we can move toward execution: the leader can now manifest the Warrior – better, the "Sustainability Warrior".

In business terms, the primary function of the Warrior is to form and execute strategy. On a more human level, the Warrior embodies passion, fearlessness, determination, commitment and focus.

The Warrior has the ability to focus all of the company's creative energies, resources and competencies into specific actions for effective output, outcomes and impact. A company has limited resources so it is essential that the company's leadership choose its activities well. As Michael Porter said: "The essence of strategy is choosing what *not* to do ... The company without a strategy is willing to try anything".[21]

The Warrior quality does not imply that the leader should take solitary top-down action. It is true that the Warrior can be manifested in autocratic leadership, for example, in terms of acute crises. But in TVC terms, the Warrior quality is not limited to the top leadership alone but should be exhibited by multiple actors within the value chain. The qualities of the Warrior can be used to mobilize collective systems leadership.

Some believe that this mobilization is "bottom-up" process; others say that systems change needs to start at the top. We have come to the conclusion that both approaches are necessary for sustainable systems change. It can start at the bottom or at the top – both approaches can be the starting point of change.

However, at one point bottom-up processes need to be accepted and facilitated by formal leaders in an organization, otherwise they will hit a "glass ceiling" and die out. Without formal support by the CEO, the chance of success is zero. Conversely, centralized leadership may well be the best starting point for successful change, but it can only succeed when employees participate in the process with a sense of co-ownership.

Francesco Starace, CEO and General Manager of Enel, explains the leadership he provided over the sustainable transition of his company:

> At the beginning of the journey, if the CEO is not the engine of this, it cannot work. The CEO must be the ultimate force behind this. But then as time goes on and the topic is established, the group that is involved and supporting it is just as important as the CEO.[22]

The most successful companies take a pragmatic approach. They realize that change leadership is an iterative process that will only yield success when efforts are persistent. Yet the Sustainability Warrior avoids force and rigidity but rather manifests flexibility and agility through a process of experimentation and constant learning.

The Sustainability Warrior, rooted in the wisdom of the other mindsets, will seek to undertake all this as a collective effort, mobilizing others to be engaged in the process. This is the systems view in action. Even though the leadership needs to be individually embodied by the leader in order to be effective, the TVC warrior fully understands the systemic nature of the problems that we are facing which require collective and systemic solutions. This can be defined as *Collective Leadership* in which both leaders and followers co-create new collective behaviors.

Integrated TVC leadership model

Returning to the TVC leadership mindsets, it is now possible to develop an integrated leadership model with a systems perspective that can drive Triple Value creation.

As a complex adaptive system, these six qualities are interdependent. Only when all six are developed to a large degree, the leadership can successfully transition from the Growth Triangle to the Cycle of Sustainability.

Generally speaking, the Warrior/Connector/Visionary/Grounder – which are four archetypes we know from classical leadership models, have a different role to play than the Wise and the Learner. On the one hand, the four classical styles provide the executive drive for the Wise and the Learner, which represent the systems perspective necessary for business sustainability today. On the other hand, the Wise and the Learner provide the meta-skills for these four classical archetypes to self-actualize.

For that reason, the Learner and the Wise form the vertical axis around which the other archetypes are positioned. The Wise and the Learner can be regarded as the source, which feed the four other archetypes when they manifest in the world.

The Visionary and the Grounder provide another (horizontal) axis driving Triple Purpose toward a regenerative system, while the Connector and the Warrior are contrasting yet complementary styles that enable the organization to operate in the larger ecosystem.

Awareness-based systems leadership

When all qualities of the leaders' awareness are dynamically balanced, they generate a strong sense of empowerment that strengthens the ability to deal with the ever-increasing levels of complexity – at the level the Self (S), the Organization (O) and System (Society/Ecosystem) (S).

This process can drive sustainable performance by the leader, his team and his entire organization. When both awareness and motivation are oriented toward addressing sustainability challenges at the highest level of complexity, the leader will have attained the highest stage of TVC leadership. At this point the leader's awareness can hold both the "outside-in" perspective required for developing a TVC strategy for his business and the "inside-out" perspective that will empower his own role as leader into taking effective action.

As mentioned, we believe that such leadership will unleash strong intrinsic motivation among co-workers. The morale and commitment of employees at work, and other stakeholders in the value chain, will grow as a result of pursuing a genuinely shared collective vision. Since employee well-being is strongly correlated to top performance, this process will initiate a virtuous cycle of personal, team, business and sustainable development – similar to what biologists would be called "regeneration", psychologist "flow" and the ancient Greek "Telus". We would call it Triple Purpose.

At this point, the value creation capacity of the firm will have reached its zenith: it will create Triple Value for its employees, the organization and society at large. This can heal the wounds caused by the distrust between business and society that characterized the era of the Growth Triangle. The company's leadership is so well-integrated with the larger system that serving the needs of the system is an expression of "enlightened self-interest". By serving others, you will also serve yourself.[23]

This is an exciting prospect: with this model, we can create a generation of business leaders who manifest as "Sustainability Warriors". These system warriors

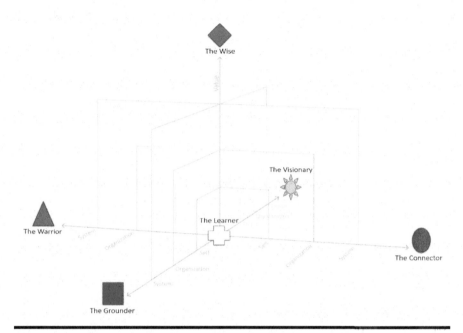

Figure 9.3 Integrated TV system mindset

can restore the distrust between business and society, while reversing environmental degradation and social inequality. They can help transform the current "competitive race" to the bottom of a lifeless planet into a "compassionate race" to the future of a flourishing society on a living vibrant earth.

Leadership example: Nelson Mandela

Nelson Mandela went through a process of self-discovery and self-empowerment when he was incarnated for 27 years, of which 18 years at Robben Island. His favorite poem was William Ernest Henley's "Invictus", which he used to recite when he felt overwhelmed by hardships: "It matters not how strait the gate. How charged with punishments the scroll, I am the master of my fate, I am the captain of my soul".[24]

The captain of the soul refers to the Learner, which Mandela unleashed in captivity. The transformative power of the Learner engendered the "inner leadership" in Mandela that prepared him for the transformative role of "outer leadership" when he was released. After being freed from Robben Island, he was capable of uniting black and white South Africa in a shared understanding of their mutual interdependency. Mandela attributed this capacity to his deep inner reflections in captivity.

This is a testimony to what can happen when the quality of the Learner is conjoined with the Wise. They empower the qualities of the Connector, Grounder, Visionary and Warrior, with superpower at systems level as a result. This is best summed up in Mandela's own words: "Our deepest fear is not that we are inadequate. Our deepest fear is that we are powerful beyond measure".[25]

Notes

1 Russell Reynolds report UN Global Compact. July 9, 2020: Retrieved from: www. russellreynolds.com/insights/thought-leadership/rra-ungc-unveil-first-of-its-kind-study-sustainable-business-leadership.
2 Mitchell, M. (2009). *Complexity: A Guided Tour*. New York: Oxford University Press
3 Lewin, K. (1997). Resolving social conflicts & field theory in social science. Washington, DC: American Psychological Association.
4 Otto, S. (2006). *Theory U – Leading from the Future as it Emerges*. Oakland, US: Berrett-Koelher.
5 Scharmer, C. O. (June 2015). "The Blind Spot: Uncovering the Grammar of the Social Field". Scharmer, C. Otto. The Blog. The Huffington Post, June 6, 2015.
6 Flavell, J. H. (1979). Metacognition and cognitive monitoring: A new area of cognitive-developmental inquiry. *American Psychologist, 34*(10), 906–911; Lutz, A., Slagter, H. A., Dunne, J. D., & Davidson, R. J. (2009). Attention regulation and monitoring in meditation. *Trends in Cognitive Sciences*. Author manuscript; available in PMC 2009 Jun 9.
7 Frankl, V. (1946). *Man's Search for Meaning*. Boston: Beacon Press.
8 Piaget, J. *The Language and Thought of the Child* (London: Routledge & Kegan Paul, 1926) [*Le Langage et la pensée chez l'enfant* (1923)].
9 See for example: Kegan and Lahey. (2009). *"Immunity to Change: How to Overcome It and Unlock the Potential in Yourself and Your Organization"*, 3–601, 249, 250, 261. Torbert, B. (2012). "Seven Transformations of Leadership". *Harvard Business Review*; Cook-Greuter, S. (1985). "A detailed description of the successive stages of ego-development". Revised December 2013; Cook-Greuter, S. R. (2004). Making the case for a developmental perspective. *Industrial and Commercial Training, 36*(7), 277–281.
10 Petrie, N. (2014). *Vertical Leadership Development: Developing Leaders for a Complex World*. Greensboro, NC: Center for Creative Leadership.
11 Whereas empathy is defined as the feeling of the suffering of others, compassion is the motivation to relieve the suffering of others. These relate to distinct neurological patterns in the brain. See for example: Singer, T., & Klimecki O. M. Empathy and Compasion, in Current Biology, September 22, 2014.
12 Hougard R. Carter, J. (2022) *Compasionate Leadership - How to do Hard Things in a Human Way*, Boston: Harvard Business Press.
13 Hougard, R., & Carter, J. (2018). *The Mind of the Leader: How to Lead Yourself, Your People, and Your Organization for Extraordinary Results*. Boston: Harvard Business Press.
14 Retrieved from: www.systemsawareness.org/project-category/generative-social-fields-initiative/.
15 Krznaric, R. (2021). *The Good Ancestor: How the Think Long Term in a Short Term World*. London: WH Allen.

16 Donnellan, L. (February 20, 2020). *Vitamix's Not-So-Secret Sauce for Success: Personal Purpose.* *Forbes* Magazine

17 Interview with Paul Polman 2011. Retrieved from: www.forumforthefuture.org/ blog/six-ways-unilever-has-achieved-success-through-sustainability-and-how-your-business-can-too.

18 Ibidem.

19 Korn Ferry. *CSO report 2020*: How sustainability leadership can unlock business resilience, innovation and future performance. Retrieved from: https://infokf.kornfe rry.com/the-rise-of-the-CSO.htm.

20 George, B. (2003). *Authentic Leadership: Rediscovering the Secrets of Creating Lasting Value.* San Francisco, CA: Jossey-Bass.

21 Porter, M. E. (1985) *The Competitive Advantage: Creating and Sustaining Superior Performance.* New York: Free Press.

22 Russell Reynolds report UN Global Compact. July 9, 2020. Retrieved from: www.russellreynolds.com/insights/thought-leadership/rra-ungc-unveil-first-of-its-kind-study-sustainable-business-leadership.

23 Tideman, S. G. (2016). *Business as an Instrument for Societal Change – In Conversation with the Dalai Lama.* Greenleaf Publications.

24 Henley, W. E. (1888). *Book of Verses*, in the section Life and Death (Echoes).

25 Nelson Mandela spoke these words at his inaugural speech as President of South Africa. Marianne Williamson wrote these words earlier in her book *A Return to Love* (1996). HarperOne.

Index

ABN AMRO Bank, 1
Accenture, 16
Accountability / accounting: accountants,
  64–65; for societal purpose, 94; national
  accounts, 73; for negative social and
  environmental impact, 102; true price, 65;
  the visionary and, 129
activist brand, 88; *see also* corporate/shareholder
  activism
adaptation, 42, 146
adult learning & development, 143
Amazon, 72
Anderson, Ray, 27, 65–66
archetypes, 121, 122, 128, 133
Arts, Muriel, 3
AT & T, 110
Awareness / aware: awakening our, 140–141;
  awareness-based learning, 115; awareness-
  based system mindset, 122; awareness-based
  system leadership, 123, 152–153; become,
  33; context-, 122–123; ecosystem awareness,
  141; field of, 114–115; inner, 125; meta-
  awareness, 141–142; outer, 124; self-, 142;
  vs thinking & feeling, 114–115; *see also*
  consciousness

B-Corps, 69
balance: optimal, 43–44; dynamic model,
  131–134
Bakker, Peter, 99, 102
Baker & McKenzie, 1
Bank of England, 19
Bayer, 62
beliefs (new & old), 51–76
Benioff, Marc, 14, 45, 87, 114, 125
Ben & Jerry, 30, 91
Berg, Jodi, 148
Bezos, Jeff, 72
Blum, Olivier, 149

Bocken, Nancy, 104
Boell, Mette, 147
Brabeck, Michael, 70–71
brand of choice, 7, 86
Brown, Patrick 93
Brundtland, Gro Harlem 55, 56, 74
Buddhism, 57
Burger King, 18
Burns, James Macgregor, 110
Business Roundtable, 28
Business and Sustainable Development
  Commission (BSDC), 16
business to society (B2S), 103–104

Cadbury, 68–69
Campbell, Joseph, 122
capitalism / capital: change from within, 2;
  credo of, 40; efficient, 72; free-market, 15;
  globalization of, 66; investment 26; power
  of capital, 65; reinvent, 99; shareholder, 65;
  stakeholder, 2
carbon / carbon adjusted earnings per share, 75
Carlsberg & Carlsberg Foundation, 88
Carney, Mark, 19
Carter, Jacqueline, 114
Catholic Church, 39
Cavendish bananas, 45
centeredness (principle of life), 42
Chevron, 18
Chief Seattle, 147
Chobani 89–90, 125, 126
Chouinard, Yvon, 87, 88
Chrysler, 74
circular economy, 2, 6, 63–64, 138
Clarke, Murphy, 112
climate change / global warming, 13, 15, 62–63,
  76, 90, 101, 145
Climate Pledge, 90
Clooney, George, 71

157